D1447379

The Day the Bunny Died

THE DAY
THE BUNNY
DIED

Victor Lownes

LYLE STUART INC.   SECAUCUS, NEW JERSEY

FIRST EDITION
Copyright © 1982, 1983 by Victor Lownes
A substantial portion of this book was
published in Great Britain by Granada
Publishing Limited under the title
Playboy Extraordinary.

All rights reserved. No part of this book
may be reproduced in any form, except by
a newspaper or magazine reviewer who wishes
to quote brief passages in connection
with a review.

Published by Lyle Stuart Inc.
120 Enterprise Ave., Secaucus, N.J. 07094
In Canada: Musson Book Company
A division of General Publishing Co. Limited
Don Mills, Ontario

Queries regarding rights and permissions should be
addressed to Lyle Stuart Inc., 120 Enterprise Avenue,
Secaucus, N.J. 07094

Library of Congress Cataloging in Publication Data

Lownes, Victor.
  The day the bunny died.

  Includes index.
  1. Lownes, Victor. 2. Businessmen—United States—
Biography. 3. Playboy Enterprises. I. Title.
HC102.5.L68A34 1983   338.7'6179 [B]   83-484
ISBN 0-8184-0340-3

MANUFACTURED IN THE UNITED STATES OF AMERICA

FOR MARILYN

ACKNOWLEDGMENTS

Writing a book at a time when, if anything, I might have preferred to forget Playboy—the magazine, the clubs, the casinos—was a difficult thing to do. Without the encouragement of my former associates, who felt the record had to be set straight, I would probably have shied away from recalling the pleasure of the days of triumph and the unfairness of the bitter, bitter end.

But even with all the encouragement there still wouldn't have been a book if it weren't for the conscientious assistance of that distinguished editor and writer Gerald McKnight. Gerald, using a cliché he'd love, bloody well kept my nose to the grindstone and the book was happily completed after all. Thanks, too, to the secretaries in Aspen and in London who helped us so much—Judith Lowe in Colorado and Susan Walker, my own former secretary at Playboy in England. Thanks too to Trudi Pacter who helped me get the book started in the first place.

For research into dates, facts and figures we looked to Group Captain Steve Stephens, Secretary of the British Casino Association. All the illustrations are from my own collection.

Nor could I forget to say thank you to all those wonderful people who worked so closely with me at Playboy, both here and in the States, to make so many years happy and successful; to name but a few—Bill Gerhauser, Arnie Morton, Dan Stone, Alan Kinghorn, Andy Wheeler, John Wintle, Linda Simmons, John Mastro, Howard Lederer, Wolf Gelderblom, John Lan, Dick Rosenzweig, and Bob

Preuss. Thanks also to our English solicitor, who was also a Playboy director and trustee, Arnold Finer, and four long-serving secretaries or, as they are properly called nowadays, personal assistants, Annie Duncan, Pat Simpson, and Loretta McCall in Chicago and Moya McGrath in London.

And, well, yes . . . Hef.

Contents

Prologue

THE FALL

The last personal communication I had from Hugh Hefner was brought to my bedside while I was recovering from having my skull cracked open while fox-hunting with the Bicester Hunt.

Hef's was one of more than a thousand cards sent by well-wishers, but I treasured it because Hef seldom writes personal notes. To have written to me at the time of my accident showed unusual kindness in him.

Hef's card had an amusing sketch on the outside of a horse in bed with a thermometer stuck in its mouth. Printed underneath was "Once upon a time there was a horse that had what you have —"

I opened the card to find the punch line: "*—They shot him!*" Underneath was the softener: "So hurry and get well." Then, in his own hand, Hef had written: "And stay away from those crazy horses!"

The card was signed "Love, Hef."

(Today the card is framed and hangs on my wall at Stocks, my country house in Aldbury, Hertfordshire, England.)

Two months later, I was fired.

Hef didn't do that job himself. He remained in his 30-room mansion in Holmby Hills area of Los Angeles with his 200 species of caged birds and sent a bird named Derick Daniels to perform the kill.

Even today I feel he owed me better than that.

11

I had worked with Hef for twenty-six years. I'd helped to build the Playboy Enterprises from a magazine pasted together on a kitchen table into an empire worth several hundred million dollars.

When I came to think about it, the nice get well card seemed almost prescient.

It wasn't that I was doing that badly for Playboy. In 1981, the casinos I managed contributed thirty-two million dollars of profit to the company. That year Playboy showed total profits of thirty-one million. In other words, all of the rest of the empire showed a net loss of one million before my profits.

The London Playboy at 45 Park Lane was the most profitable casino in the world.

Why then would Hefner fire me?

People do strange things when they panic. It seems to me that Hef panicked. There is no other rational explanation. Acting in a frenzy of fear, and at his bidding, his executives became executioners. There was a loss of perspective in the palace.

And, as with the French revolution, many of the executives who judged and condemned me were themselves soon guillotined.

Playboy's president Derick Daniels and vice presidents Don Parker and Lee Templeton and several others were soon to join the ranks of America's unemployed.

That day, April 15, 1981, might well be commemorated as the beginning of the end of the Playboy empire.

The day the bunny died.

My fractured skull, caused when my horse slipped and fell on an icy road, severed my olfactory nerve. It caused me to lose forever all sense of smell. In view of what was to come, perhaps that was a good thing.

After my firing, I couldn't resist giving Hefner a little dig. I sent a photograph of the get-well card with a note attached. "Remember this card?" I wrote. "It seems strangely prophetic ... *or did you know*?" I never got an answer. But then I guess things between the two of us had been wearing thin for quite some time. And when thinking about it, as I did the other day while relaxing in my jacuzzi after a strenuous day's fox-hunting, I realize I have had a lot of life's good things and many tremendously satisfying experiences to thank Hefner and Playboy for.

Events should prove that he made a terrible blunder. Still, how can I feel anything but gratitude for the man whose genius and drive originated the whole concept on which we thrived at Playboy? How can one not admire the way Hefner reflected and legitimized the changing mores of English-speaking society?

His was the belief that we must move away from the hypocritical and puritanical notion that all material wealth and self-indulgence are in some way sinful. He made his move towards a more open "let's enjoy it" existence against much opposition—and a whole new generation cheered.

Hugh Hefner, of course, would say that he had sound business reasons for letting me go. I can't get inside the man's mind, and when he telephoned me that night from California I was too shocked and numb with sleep to listen. The call reached me at four a.m.; I'd taken a sleeping pill to knock me out. Without it, I couldn't have slept. With it, I couldn't take in what Hefner was saying by way of justification. I fell asleep and woke some time later to see the receiver dangling on its cord.

"Victor," some remote part of my numbed brain remembered him saying across the fact-blurring distance of those six thousand miles, "you've got to understand ..."

As my mind cleared and I took a look in the mirror at the face which had launched, if not a thousand, certainly scores of Clubs, I told myself the unbelievable, unthinkable truth was that I was no longer Britain's "playboy extraordinary," the man Hugh Hefner had entrusted with running the entire lucrative British end of his business and put in charge of all Playboy hotels, clubs and casinos throughout the world. Next to him, I had been one of the most influential executives in the company and the most consistently successful in bringing home the bacon.

There was much no one could take from me.

The life I had selected for myself was unique in combining pleasure with industry. In London, I had watched over those green-baize tables where millions of pounds were won and lost. I had personally designed the ambience and magic of the club in London's Park Lane and similarly the subtle shifts in décor, costumes and menus of the top-of-the-market Clermont and near-bottom-of-the-market Victoria Sporting Club.

Organizing the recruiting and to an extent "fathering" the parade of gorgeous young girls who came to work for me as cocktail bunnies and croupier bunnies was one of the more enjoyable parts of the job. It was also the most widely misunderstood. I had to be careful not to do anything which in today's world might be considered sexual harassment.

Nevertheless, I didn't have to work at acquiring the reputation as a playboy of the Western world. The combination of being a single man who regularly dated some of the most beautiful girls in England and of being the captain of the Playboy Club, itself a ship of fantasies, was enough to guarantee that image.

I suppose, in a way, you could say that my lifestyle was in keeping with Hefner's carefully delineated Playboy philosophy. Mine was not by any means a copy of Hefner's own lifestyle, but I lived a socially acceptable nonconformist pattern that allowed me to choose the kind of pleasures and adventures that suited my own taste. My position with Playboy didn't require me to live up to someone else's idea of proper "executive image" as it might at National Cash Register or IBM.

In my country home, in some ways I came closer to a model of an eighteenth-century English fox-hunting squire than the popular idea of a playboy. I took my life in the English countryside seriously. But I didn't get myself pigeon-holed that way either. Riding to hounds, frolicking in the jacuzzi, or flying my own helicopter were recreations I enjoyed and truly felt I'd earned. The parties, the beautiful girls, the constant gossip-column write-ups (true and false), all made my life sound like nothing but a spirited romp, whereas that was only a fraction of the story.

"Hef needs you," I was told on all sides. "He's never forgotten what you did for him in the early days." If that was true, he must have had a momentary lapse of memory when, twenty-seven years after our initial meeting, I was shoved out of his company and his life without so much as a face-to-face discussion. Had there been one, things might have ended differently for both of us.

Chapter One
A NEW BEGINNING

I first met Hugh Hefner soon after he'd started *Playboy*. Hef and I became close friends. He hired me in 1955 as Special Projects Director for the magazine. Later I was promoted to Circulation Promotion Director and Advertising Promotion Director and made a vice president. I used to go around making speeches about the kind of schlock advertising we wouldn't accept in the magazine—all those crummy mail order ads. We only accepted high-class stuff. I think this selective concept saved *Playboy* from becoming just another publishing flash-in-the-pan.

The night we were introduced, I was in an unsettled state of mind. It was only a few months since I'd walked out on my wife and two children and had lost interest in my job. Indeed, because of my marriage separation, which immediately made me eligible to be drafted into the peacetime US Army, I no longer had a job. My grandfather's industrial security and time lock firm didn't want rising executives who might be yanked out at any time.

One thing I did have—and, as I quickly discovered, so did Hefner—was a wide-eyed enthusiasm for the company of attractive young women, particularly those receptive to the fun and games aspects of the "new morality."

Until then and nearly all the way through my seven and a half years of marriage and the birth of our two children (my son, Victor, whom we called Val, was four and Meredith Ann just two), I'd lived a faithful, respectable bourgeois married life. Two things had happened to break open this chrysalis.

Firstly, my firm sent me from Chicago, where we lived, to New York for a whole summer of special management training. I must admit that the bright lights of New York overwhelmed this youthful midwesterner. I went out on the town practically every night: fine restaurants, theatre, nightclubs. It was all very exciting. Well, at least as exciting as it could be on a limited budget.

This was in 1953; the birth control pill was becoming accepted and old attitudes were changing. It was the first time since my marriage in 1946, when I was only eighteen, that I had dated around. And I was surprised and delighted at the reception I was getting.

I'd never imagined I was attractive—certainly not *that* attractive—to women. It taught me a lot about myself; well, perhaps more about the new sexual freedom and how it was changing boy-girl relations.

I had a room in the Tudor Hotel in Tudor City, near the United Nations Building, and I had little trouble coaxing the girls I dated up to my tiny room, even though it contained no TV, no radio, no etchings. There was little more by way of promised entertainment than me and a small single bed.

It was this sudden introduction to the joys of sex outside marriage, and a love affair which began here, which really broke up our marriage. I felt, suddenly, that I'd been living in a trap all these years, despite the very comfortable and acceptable life my wife Judy and I shared.

One night I saw mention of a little club called RSVP in an article in *Park East* magazine, written by A. C. Spectorsky. I went there and was enchanted by the singer, Mable Mercer. Mabel at fifty-three was no spring chicken. She was a half-English, half-American chanteuse, not anyone's idea of a glamorous, torchy nightclub entertainer. She sat in a chair in a most dignified manner while she sang. But she had a way of expressing the lyrics of the songs as if they were poetry.

Hers wasn't a great voice, but she made each of the words tell, stretching some and throwing away others. It got right through to me. I liked her so much I went to the club nearly every night; and as Mabel would sing them, I'd mouth the words of songs like Cole Porter's "Looking At You" or Bart Howard's "Fly Me to the Moon" in the ear of some girl I fancied. I'd get the credit for Mabel Mercer's beautifully expressed sincerity.

This either turned them on so that they'd practically drag me out of the club and up to my room, or I'd know we weren't on the same wavelength. If any girl tossed her head and pointed out that Mabel couldn't sing, I knew she missed the poetry and was listening only for the song.

Mabel didn't pull large crowds but she attracted interesting people. I recall one particular evening when I glanced around the room and recognized the Duke and Duchess of Windsor, Nat King Cole, Frank Sinatra and his then-wife, Ava Gardner. Mabel Mercer had a great effect on Sinatra. When "the new Sinatra" made his first album he sent Mabel a telegram: "Listen to my new album and you'll hear yourself." She'd taught him to make the lyrics as meaningful as the music, which was her way. And it became Frank Sinatra's "my way."

The magic lasted. Suddenly I'd been immersed in sexual freedom. After the summer had ended and I went back to my home and family in Evanston, Illinois, I carried with me memories of a lifestyle I'd never dreamed possible.

My one serious extra-marital experience occurred at this time. It was with a married, but separated, woman, about ten years my senior, née Nelrose Durfee. She had scrapped the rural-sounding first name of Nelrose for the more sophisticated-sounding Irene. An easterner, she was in Chicago undergoing psychoanalysis.

I was in a bar having a drink with a friend when she caught my eye. Looking at her picture now, I wonder what it was about her, but whatever it was it knocked me out.

I asked her to have a drink—something I'd never done with a stranger and would be unlikely to do even now. She smiled acceptance, we got talking, and pretty soon I was in bed in her apartment. More than any other sensation, I felt surprised as hell that it had all been such a piece of cake. It never occurred to me that I was the one who'd been seduced.

Irene had light brown hair and a fine figure. She had travelled widely with her husband, a wealthy member of the clan which owned the Lerner shops. I thought she was fabulous.

Then suddenly she disappeared. I was so besotted with her I went to her shrink and signed up. I thought he'd either cure me of my obsession about her or tell me where I could find her. He did neither. He claimed professional ethics forbade him even to concede he knew her. It was a girlfriend of hers who finally told me that Irene was in a hotel in New Haven, Connecticut.

I walked in on her while she was having dinner in the hotel restaurant with a young Yale student. There was quite a scene, but I managed to persuade her to leave him sitting there and go with me back to her hotel room. She could see I was desperate. Maybe the *frisson* of having aroused me to the extent where I would chase her halfway across America made her feel good.

We made love until the wee small hours. Then I looked out into the square. Good Lord, four in the morning and there was the boy she'd been having dinner with sitting on a bench, his head in his hands. He was as crazy about her as I was. *I could see myself!*

It was the last I ever saw of her. The sight of that pathetic young man sitting out there in the cold turned me off and I walked out of her life. But she was a major reason why Judy and I separated: Irene convinced me that there were far more exciting ways of spending one's youth and life than monogamously sitting behind expensive drapes in a fashionable suburb watching the kids grow up and mowing the lawn on Sundays.

I'd married too young to know what I really wanted from life or where I was heading. Too young to even fully know myself. Now, at twenty-five, I was trapped in the world of tennis clubs—ours was in smart, suburban Evanston—folk music (Judy's specialty at the University of Chicago where we'd met had been jazz, publishing a national magazine called *Jazz Quarterly,* and lunatic left-wing politics and lost causes), and for me, boredom.

"You behave as if you'd only just woken up to being alive," a girl in New York had told me one passionate night. "Where have you been?" Wherever it was, I saw it was not where I wanted to be from now on. It made me wonder why I'd ever married in the first place.

Not that Judy Downs lacked any of the qualities of a first-class wife. She was as eligible as any princess: a peachlike beauty who'd won second place in a Miss Arkansas contest, and had brains and vitality to go with her looks. Also her family had money, they owned a large seed rice plantation and Angus Cattle ranch, which made her a very up-market young lady indeed.

My family was comfortably well-off, but they never gave me anything except a super education. Judy's parents presented me with my first automobile, a 1946 De Soto, as a wedding present and they paid for our house.

It still wasn't a good idea to tie myself to the prettiest girl on the campus, a virgin, when I had yet to understand myself and the changing world in which I was growing up. When I look back over the way we came together, it seems to me I'd tumbled into wedlock rather thoughtlessly.

Judy played the saxophone along with the piano and guitar and I'd stupidly been party to getting her sax—a very good Selmer Padless—lost. What had happened was that a great jazz player of the twenties, Voltaire (Volly) Defoe, an alcoholic, borrowed it with my help. And he lost it, or pawned it to buy drink. God, what a mess that was, but trying to find it brought Judy and me closer together.

At eighteen the search for a lost saxophone was enough to seal the bond. You can't just walk away after losing one of a girl's favorite possessions, can you? Well, especially if she's just about the prettiest girl on campus.

So here I was, seven years later, suddenly aware that the world held many fascinating and sexually stimulating girls just as exciting as the one I was married to—and each one having the additional quality of being a novelty; *ergo* ego booster. I was depressingly sure that the future held little more comfort for me than a well-padded cell which I was building myself.

I didn't have much money of my own, aside from the salary of around $10,000 a year I was paid by my grandfather's Silent Watchman Corporation. My father had died in 1950 after years of battling TB, leaving me only an *Encyclopedia Britannica,* a broken watch, and a pair of newly purchased pajamas he'd never lived to wear. The bulk of his modest estate went to my mother.

The breaking point came unexpectedly. We'd asked some friends over for the evening. "You know, darling," Judy announced, "*the* Wesley Baylors. *Your* friends." I began to see that I was going out of my way to encourage socially significant people who were not terribly interesting. Why? Chicago in those days, and probably still today, had many snobs and social climbers—and I, pickaxe in hand, was putting on my crampons.

Our guests arrived with a vast collection of color slides they'd taken on a recent holiday in the Bahamas. "We know you'll *adore* these," Wes's wife gushed. "Wes is such a *brilliant* photographer, and he just couldn't stop taking pictures, it was all so beautiful."

After dinner, our enraptured friends showed us their collection. It was agony. I sat staring at the never-ending succession of projected slides and wondering how to contain my boredom, sleepiness and near-paralysis. If this was suburban excitement I was in big trouble. It hit me with intensity that this was a foretaste of what lay ahead if I was to stay locked into this existence. I had to break out.

Next day Judy was chilly at breakfast. Maybe she'd noticed. She already suspected I'd been veering off the rails. A telephone call from one of the girls I'd been with in New York had alerted her. But also my obvious lack of interest in my own friends the previous night had set off an alarm. She sensed that I was rejecting the pattern of our stiff-collared respectability.

"What time will you be home for dinner?" she asked as I brushed her cheek with my lips on my way out. The question was innocent enough. But in my state of mind it had the ring of a prison regulation. "I can't make dinner tonight," I told her. "I won't be home for dinner."

I saw her stiffen. "In that case," she said in a small, tight voice, "don't bother to come home at all."

I laughed and said "Okay" and drove off. Much later I called and told her I'd thought about it seriously and I'd decided to mean it. I never went home again.

For the first few months of our separation I lived in the Park Dearborn Hotel on Chicago's near north side. Then I found an apartment on nearby North Wells Street which suited my idea of a bachelor life. It was one enormous, high-ceilinged room with a series of fake Old Masters hanging on the walls, and its special attraction was that I could afford the place and still have enough left over to enjoy myself.

Even that might have been out of reach if Judy had looked to me for more in the way of financial support than she did. In fact, she has always turned away from any effort I've made to be patronizingly generous. Seven years ago, when I sent her a check for a thousand dollars to buy herself something to commemorate our thirtieth wedding anniversary, she sent it back with a note I treasure.

"I simply don't have a category in my budget system for contributions from ex-husbands ..." she wrote me. "Please accept my deep gratitude for the kindness, consideration and helpfulness you have consistently given. You have just received the intercontinental, interplanetary, intergalactic EX-HUSBAND OF THE CENTURY award...."

I framed the check and letter together and hung them in my hallway, where ever since they have brought tears to the eyes of my men friends who have costly divorce problems. How could anybody be so lucky? But then Judy always was a high-minded, sweet and generous girl. A wife just didn't fit into my concept of life in the fast lane—no room in the sports car, so to speak.

Oh yes, I was more than making up for all the time lost watching slides and mowing lawns. The apartment at 1311 North Wells contained a draped-off recess in the wall where the bed was: an ideal arrangement. Many of the girls I was consoling myself with seemed to think so too.

The place had a tiny kitchen, excellent for throwing a succession of small parties. I had become involved with a crowd of people, mostly in showbusiness, who liked enjoying themselves. They were stimulating and attractive with none of the dreary affectations I'd escaped from in Evanston. Before long I found myself involved in the entertainment world myself.

It's possible I've inherited showbusiness flair from my mother, whose family ran movie theatres, because almost as soon as I was free of my job and family responsibilities I risked my small savings as an "angel." I brought the immortal Mabel Mercer to Chicago for a concert in a nightclub, the Blue Angel, and it was a great success, a sell-out.

While I taped her performance, my partner, a local radio disc jockey, Jay Trompeter, worked the sound system. I had hired a photographer, Mike Shea, to take the pictures. He turned out to be a man I instinctively liked.

Indeed Mike enjoyed life almost as much as I did, and after the concert we became good friends. But I'd no idea he was going to be influential in changing my life.

It was Mike Shea who brought Hugh Hefner along to a party I gave for comedian Jonathan Winters and introduced us.

As always, there were plenty of pretty girls present. I'd been dating a dancer, Mary Ann La Joie, from the show at the Empire Room of the Palmer House Hotel where Winters was topping the bill. She roomed with another dancer, Shirley Delancey. Since the party was in Jonathan Winters's honor, I'd invited most of the show's dancers and musicians.

Mike Shea had asked me beforehand if I minded if he brought "That guy who runs the new magazine, *Playboy,* Hugh Hefner." I hadn't met Hefner, but I'd modelled for the magazine and I knew, because Mike had told me, that the new publication was really taking off.

The pictures Mike had shot of me were to illustrate an article on the "flying executive"—the white collar stereotype using jets as a form of inter-office transportation. It hardly occurred to me that an article so basically serious fitted into what I took to be the character of the *Playboy* magazine I'd glimpsed on newsstands.

I'd never actually bought a copy. I suffered from (and still am inhibited by) a curious sort of shyness, or sensitivity, which sometimes holds me back from asking a druggist for anything as self revealing as athlete's foot powder.

The semi-nudes in *Playboy* scared me off buying it the couple of times I'd picked up and glanced at copies on the newsstands. I didn't want a newsdealer to know that I dug that kind of stuff. On the other hand, I was also drawn to the sort of informative articles like the one I'd helped to illustrate and to the magazine's fiction by leading authors advertised on its cover.

The night that I met Hef, I didn't fully understand his editorial concept. I didn't see that Hefner had brilliantly sensed the need for a magazine that young men, upper income and better educated young men, could call "my magazine"—a magazine that unembarrassedly reflected the New Morality.

My thought, when Shea introduced us, was that this slim, dark guy who looked like a college student must be living a life no Reilly had ever aspired to. It didn't surprise me that he was wearing white socks—obviously too busy with all that parade of glamour waltzing through his life to be fashion-conscious. It was not for some time that I learned he *liked* white socks. Indeed, that his taste in clothes was as undergraduate and unsophisticated as his average reader's— the post-war college student and young executive.

But what I also learned was that Hugh Hefner was a highly intelligent, switched-on character with a mind-blowing belief in his personal destiny, and in his magazine. It turned out, too, that we

shared many things. The night of the party he brought one girl with
him, the magazine's famous Subscription Manager, Janet Pilgrim
(who was twice to be featured as Playmate—itself some kind of
record). Even so, he was soon chatting up Shirley, Mary Ann's
room-mate. So this, too, helped to bring us together.

Hefner didn't leave the party until three in the morning, by which
time I'd got to know more about him. He'd started his magazine
because he'd seen what revealing pictures of girls could do for sales
when he had a job with a magazine called *Modern Man,* following
his start in the circulation department of *Esquire.*

Came the time when *Esquire* was moving from Chicago to New
York, Hefner asked for a raise of five dollars a week to go with
them. When they failed to agree that he was worth a five dollar
raise, he quit. He scraped together $600. With a few more hundreds
in loans, he started *Playboy* in his own kitchen, naming it after a
make of sports car then struggling to get into production. *Playboy*
was originally going to be called *Stag Party.* It's logo was to be a
stag with antlers. Another men's magazine named *Stag* objected and
thus was *Playboy* chosen and history made.

By the night of my party in 1954, its sales were rocketing with
every issue. "On the first issue we put out," he told me, "we
omitted the date [December 1953] so that, if copies didn't sell right
away, it could stay on the newsstands until they did." With the
calendar picture of Marilyn Monroe in the centerfold, and another of
her on the cover, he was certainly hedging his bets. Even with a print
run of 50,000, you couldn't buy a copy of that issue days after it hit
the few newsstands which would carry a new and daring magazine.

Hefner told me: "I had to find those centerfold pictures at a price
I could pay." How he'd done it, he told me, was to buy them from a
calendar company which owned the rights to the poses and pay them
$75 each to reprint them in a magazine format.

All in all, it was impressive. The man plainly had the world by the
tail, and it was the same world I wanted to get into. I decided to do a
little impressing on my own account. I explained about the singer
I'd brought to Chicago for a concert and told him about her

aphrodisiac effect on young ladies. "Just listen to these tapes," I suggested, "and tell me if you don't think Mabel Mercer sells a lyric great."

When he'd listened a while, Hef nodded, "She's got something," he told me. "Why don't you write a piece about her for my magazine?"

Why not? I'd written a few small pieces for the jazz journal my wife Judy had published while we were at the University of Chicago together. I had plenty I wanted to say about Mabel. In my estimation, Mercer's way of singing, from the heart and soul, had never been given the tribute it deserved. Her songs were emotional sermons, reaching deep inside, touching and stroking the memories and cravings everyone had.

"Fine," I said. "I'd like to do that. Let's have dinner and discuss it." I didn't tell Hefner I hadn't ever read his magazine, or that I had no more than a hazy idea of his policy of blending good, seriously written articles with the pin-ups.

So it was arranged. Later he asked me to write an article on Jonathan Winters, whom he'd met at my party and who was the kind of fast-rising talent *Playboy* liked to introduce to its readers. It got through to me that Hefner, who had a most intense and concentrated gaze (not unlike, as I was to discover, Frank Sinatra's), was a man who used his intuitive flair to make rapid decisions. He knew what he wanted and was quickly bored by what he didn't want.

Since I was much the same, I began to look at him with a respect and awe which I was careful not to reveal too openly. He'd studied psychology at the University of Illinois, so I thought it wise to be guarded, even though we were obviously getting along well. I noted his pronounced, somewhat strange addiction for Pepsi-Cola–never Coca-Cola, for some reason known only to him.

And I noticed, too, how enthusiastic he could become towards any subject or viewpoint which he thought fitted into *Playboy*, his guidebook for the young urban man, and which, at the same time, added to his personal lifestyle. To him, I believe, I seemed a slight jump ahead in worldliness and sophistication. (A. C. Spectorsky, the writer whose article led me to Mabel Mercer, later became the guiding editorial genius at *Playboy.* He used to kid about the fact that "Hefner listens to everyone but when Lownes talks Hef sees it all in technicolor.")

Some nights later, Hef and I met at a small place near his office, where there was a restaurant upstairs and dancing downstairs. My understanding of the man, his commitment to a liberated lifestyle in which pleasure and excellence combined, grew as we talked.

In November 1955, when Hugh Hefner offered me a job on the magazine, I didn't hesitate to accept. We had known each other for over a year. We had discussed my promotional ideas and those had seemed promising to Hef. Together we shared good times and we were dating room-mates Mary Ann La Joie and Shirley Delancey. I for one had found what I truly felt would be a lifelong friend.

Chapter Two
NO DRAFT FOR VICTOR

I really wanted the job Hefner offered me on that November evening in 1955. There was a problem. I was waiting to be drafted into the Army.

The Korean war was over, so this meant going into the peacetime Army. I couldn't see the point if it meant giving up an exciting new job. Neither could president Eisenhower. I was relieved to learn that the president had a bill lying on his desk waiting for his signature, which exempted all men over twenty-six from being called up—and I was twenty-seven.

Unfortunately, the president was in the hospital recovering from a heart attack. There seemed to be no way I could get a deferment until he returned to his desk and signed the darned thing. And after three nail-biting months—during which I worked for Hef and his team on a temporary basis—my time had run out. Eisenhower's bill still hadn't been made law, and I had received orders to report for duty. There seemed no way I could avoid my fate.

Hef threw a splendid farewell party for me in the coach house where I was now spending my last civilian days. A friend brought a couple of girls to the party. Madeline Smith was one of them and she made quite an impression on me. I didn't bother to ask for her phone number because I knew that Eldon Sellers, the fellow *Playboy* executive I was now sharing the coach house with, had managed to nail it down.

By the Monday after the party, I faced my last two days of freedom. I thought to myself, what the hell! I'll have one more try to get myself out of this. I put a call through to the head of my draft board, a prominent Chicago lawyer.

He wasn't there when I called his office, but the woman who answered the phone had a very familiar voice. She sounded, in fact, just like the attractive girl at my send-off party, Madeline Smith.

I rang off and buzzed Eldon Sellers's office. "What is Madeline's work number?" I asked him. He told me. Sure enough, it was the number I'd just called.

I rang her back. This time, I told her who I was and why I had called. "Madeline," I said, "I'm trying to talk your boss into giving me a six-month deferment." There was a pause, then she took me completely by surprise.

"Don't worry," she said easily. "I'll get you your deferment."

"How on earth can you be so sure?" I asked. She wouldn't say. Maybe, I thought, she's just one of those super secretaries, whose bosses let them run the office, hmmm? In any event, she called me back to say it was OK. No draft for Victor.

As soon as I received my deferment, I sent a case of wine to her boss. Then I invited her and a girlfriend to a weekend at a summer resort in Indiana. She accepted and I asked Hefner along to make a foursome. We all had a wonderful time. I couldn't believe my luck—no draft *and* Madeline.

When I joined *Playboy,* the offices were in an old grey-painted townhouse on Chicago's near northside. On one side of us was a Salvation Army headquarters, and across the street was the Holy Name Cathedral. Neither establishment exactly approved of Playboy.

But then, in its early days, hardly *anyone* approved of *Playboy.* The Post Office and the FBI were constantly looking for ways to trip us up. They nearly succeeded more than once.

Our pin-up pictures, by today's standards, were very tame indeed. You rarely saw a nipple. You never saw a full frontal nude. But there was one exception. As part of a travel lay-out on "What To Do in Chicago," we ran a picture of a strip joint in Cicero, the suburb where Al Capone made his headquarters.

The picture featured a totally naked stripper. Because it was believed to be against the law to run a full frontal in those days, we made sure the picture was very tiny: postage stamp size, in fact. Even with a magnifying glass nobody could be quite sure whether or not the stripper was wearing a "G" string. I suggested we take no chances. We published the photo unretouched in the magazine. Then I suggested to photo editor Vince Tajiri that it would be wise if they got out the negative and drew a thin G-string line on the girl. They did, and we made a new negative for our files. The original was thrown out.

A few weeks later the FBI came round to our offices, demanding to see the negative. With great pleasure we obliged. They lost interest when the retouched negative showed a G-string—which points up the absurdity of censorship. What the reader *saw* was unchanged, but presumably we would have been prosecuted if the *negative* had indicated full frontal nudity.

The early days of *Playboy* were heady, exciting and very hardworking. Hefner and I worked harder and longer than anyone else—often until three in the morning. Hefner's marriage was in the process of breaking up. During the week he lived in a bedroom behind his office, going home weekends to Milly and their two children.

Hefner and I were both discovering and enjoying the new sexual freedom which we were pioneering in the magazine. Both of us had the same taste in girls—we were interested in quantity as well as quality. And neither of us wanted to get married again, which made us even more popular with the girls, because they regarded us as something of a challenge.

Most evenings Hef and I would finish work at midnight and then go on the prowl in the neighborhood bars. We'd drink whisky, talk endlessly and, of course, pick up girls. Sometimes, if we were working really late on the magazine, we'd have our girlfriends come in to us. They'd sit around on the sofas reading magazines, waiting until we were ready to go out and play.

When Hefner's divorce became final, he really came into his own as a playboy. Both Hef and I adopted the same routine. We would always have a number one girlfriend, who would publicly be seen to be our property. Then we'd have a few spares in the background.

One night he came in to find me fast asleep on the office floor. I'd been working round the clock. He was impressed although he long before knew that I, like he, was totally committed to the magazine.

Outside the office we seemed a carefree pair. His interest in Mary Ann La Joie's room-mate, Shirley Delancey, had developed and I was still seeing a lot of Mary Ann. At other times, when an opportunity presented itself, we'd find other partners.

There were plenty of girls who got a big kick out of spending an evening or whole night with youthful executives from *Playboy* magazine, which everyone knew was taking off fast. Hef had the additional advantage, in their minds, of being the man who decided which girl would grace the centerfold, though, in fact, he always tried to be objective in making his decision.

We had other things on our minds besides girls, of course. It was easy for me to pitch the magazine's glamorous sales figures at prospective advertisers, but convincing them that anything as apparently light-hearted and liberated could sell their products as well as *Time* and *Newsweek* was another matter.

We were unique. I knew this partly from the letters coming in from colleges all over America and partly from the way the stuff we plugged or advertised in *Playboy* sold. The big hurdle was getting this across to a staid, prejudiced hardcore of advertisers and their agents in the Big League, such as the multi-million-dollar tobacco, alcohol and menswear manufacturers.

From experience I'd picked up as the Chesterfield cigarette campus rep, I hit on an idea. With Hefner's agreement, we ran an ad in *Playboy* at the start of the school year, canvassing for recruits among the student population to act as our representatives, such as I had been. The difference, as Hefner shrewdly saw, was that we needed to offer no money, not even the measly few dollars a month I had been paid. A free subscription to *Playboy* was enough, with a few bonus payment incentives for success in persuading local outfitters to carry a display for *Playboy's* advertisers in their windows or inside their store. We got more applicants than we could use.

I set them to work, concentrating primarily on clothing, because early on, both tobacco and alcohol accounts showed resistance to our sales story. There was an association of clothing manufacturers, the National Association of Retail Clothiers and Furnishers (NARCF), which held annual conventions. This gave me a great opportunity to put *Playboy* across.

All centerfold girls whose photographs appeared as Playmates were under contract to make personal appearances on the magazine's behalf. I dressed them in cheerleader-style black sweaters— with the white bunny trademark on the back—white flared skirts, and sophisticated high-heeled black shoes. At the next NARCF convention I had them unabashedly signing their photos in the magazines for queues of menswear manufacturers and retailers, and giving stimulating appeal to the magazine. At the same time, I and my staff were busy presenting the hard evidence of *Playboy's* pulling power, both in the colleges and outside. Thus did we break into our first major advertising area.

Not all the menswear ads we ran were as entertaining as one ad I remember. It was for the Springmaid Sheet Company. It pictured an exhausted Indian in a hammock watched over by an Indian maid, with the caption: "A buck well spent on a Springmaid sheet"—but the fact that we sold advertising to some major manufacturers was all I cared about.

What Hefner and I were mainly concerned with was selling the *Playboy* image. We knew from the polls (which Gallup and others were regularly taking) that—to the surprise of many—we were topping the figures of the old standards, such as *Time, Newsweek* and *Esquire,* on the very important college campuses. The job was to get this message across to advertisers whose conservative attitudes might seem strange in view of the fact that cigarette and alcohol manufacturers cater to permissive markets.

Playboy could be, and was, the most successful magazine to be launched post-war in the United States, but still the old-timers among the cigarette and liquor advertisers—which was most of them—refused to consider a magazine with semi-nude girls' photographs displayed inside. Something else was needed to get through to them.

Four years after I'd joined him, Hef ran a piece in the magazine about the delights of a Chicago nightspot called the Gaslight. The Gaslight used the gimmick of giving each member a key to the place. By now we'd moved to larger premises in a converted warehouse building and Hef had a spacious office. We were a long way from the days when his printer had objected to the butter stains on copy he sent down from his kitchen table when he had edited the magazine at home.

As his Promotion Director, I kept close tabs on the mail our articles inspired. This one on the Gaslight was phenomenal. We had more than 3,000 letters sent in by guys wanting to know how they could become members of Gaslight even though the article mentioned that a key cost $25.00. I saw that our readers were probably the best market in the world for such an attraction.

Hef was in his office. I went and showed him the figure. "Look at this," I said. "Don't you think we should be doing something like this ourselves? We have the audience out there. And a Playboy Club would fit in perfectly with the image we're trying to create."

I could see the Club in my mind, even as I said it. Hef had made a unique breakthrough by presenting photographs of girls as beautiful and lightly clad as the drawings *Esquire* had been featuring in sketches for years. The Club could be an exciting new step forward.

A Club could be tied to the same fantasy as the magazine. It could offer the eye-pleasing ambience of gorgeous girls as waitresses and provide solid proof that we were reaching the alcohol and tobacco consuming market. Where Hef had been operating on a brilliant but wholly intuitive flair, I had the advantage of three years spent studying Business Administration, after I'd earned my BA degree, at the University of Chicago. All of my training and all my instincts told me that the Playboy Club idea would be a winner.

"I agree," Hefner said. "Let's look into it."

The more we talked and studied the pros and cons, the more attractive the idea became. We were in the middle of these discussions when I pushed another idea Hefner also became keen about, a jazz festival. By now I'd brought restaurateur Arnold Morton into the organization. Hef had hired Bob Preuss as our financial and business manager. Preuss had been his room-mate at the University of Illinois. Howard Lederer, a great advertising sales director, was hired in New York. Our strength was growing.

We were all enthusiastic about the festival. It would be a showcase for another advertising market—hi-fi and records. The problem—and it was a tough one—was locating a suitable available hall for the massive bill and even more massive attendance we were sure that our promotion in *Playboy* would attract. We had our eye on Soldiers Field. We thought we had it and then were disappointed. The Roman Catholic Church in Chicago, no friends of *Playboy*, had objected. Then the Stockyards Arena was also ruled out by the owners. We were in trouble.

Fortunately Arthur Wirtz, a big Chicago real estate man, heard of our search. Wirtz's extensive holdings included the Chicago Stadium. I don't think for one moment that Wirtz himself believed, as we did, that we could fill such a vast arena in the middle of August when most Chicagoans liked to spend their leisure time outdoors. But our faith in *Playboy* and its pulling power made us take it on. And Arthur Wirtz was to witness a minor miracle.

We gave the Playboy Jazz Festival maximum advertising in the magazine. This, we announced, would be "the biggest jazz festival ever held anywhere in the world." Actually, that was an understatement. I flew to Newport, Rhode Island, to study the techniques

George Wein used to promote his famous Newport Jazz Festival. Impressive as they were, I thought *Playboy* could do better.

One of the problems with Newport was the long interval that elapsed between each act—dragging down the excitement created by the bands. I flew back to Chicago thinking up ways to overcome this problem.

Hefner, who was taking an active interest in the festival and suggesting many of the name bands and singers for it, was in his office. I told him what I had thought of on the plane. "It's going to need a revolving stage," I said. "That way we can have one orchestra setting up while another is playing—then switch them around without losing a second's playing time."

Hefner looked dubious. I could see that he was considering the cost. Everything rested on the power of *Playboy* to pull in crowds of 23,000 for each of the five scheduled performances, two afternoons and three nights. I'd estimated that we needed capacity crowds every night, and I reckoned on substantial numbers for the matinées.

Hef brightened, however, when I told him that we had been successful in booking most of the acts which he had suggested. There was hardly a name band or famous singer not included: Louis Armstrong, Duke Ellington, Count Basie, Red Nichols, Stan Kenton and Dizzie Gillespie. Among the vocalists were Ella Fitzgerald, Peggy Lee, Nina Simone, June Christie and Bobby Darin.

As a special attraction I'd made arrangements with the Chicago Police Department to lend us a fifty-strong posse of their officers.

One stunt I worked out was to replace an unobtainable Frank Sinatra with a simple but effective substitute. He worked sensationally well. A singer, Duke Hazlett, was the spitting image of Sinatra. I hired him. In a blaze of searchlights, I had the police detachment march bravely on with Hazlett—carrying a raincoat tossed casually over his shoulder and wearing a felt hat in Sinatra style.

Hazlett not only looked like Sinatra, he sang like him. His

rendition of the song "Come Fly with Me" could have fooled anyone.

To avoid deception, I had Mort Sahl announce at the end of his number that Hazlett was an imitator. But Hazlett was so good that a lot of people believed he was really Sinatra. In fact, one of the morning newspapers covering the show reported Sinatra's smash-hit performance.

The show was an enormous triumph. There has never been, and never will be, a jazz show like it. Every performance sold out. If Hefner, always a dedicated liberal, hadn't donated the entire first-day's proceeds to the National Association for the Advancement of Colored People, we'd have made a profit.

As it was, the Jazz Festival cost us only $50,000, which, in view of our having had to pay ten grand each to Armstrong and Ella, didn't seem outrageous to me. Anyway, it brought golden publicity to *Playboy.*

Furthermore, when we later came under pressure to show there was no racial discrimination in our Clubs, that donation to the NAACP assured us of many friends who would speak up on Playboy's behalf and properly support us as a fair-minded company.

Our triumph convinced me we could overcome all difficulties in opening and running a club of our own—a "Playboy Club." Arnie Morton and I began to go more seriously into the whole idea. The Playboy offices were now at 232 East Ohio Street, and that was where most of the planning was done. We worked with Hefner on into the night. The days were never long enough. Starting an entirely new project, yet blending it in with the Playboy image created in the magazine, called for enormous organization and attention to every detail.

We now had A. C. (Augie) Spectorsky editing *Playboy* magazine. He was the journalist whose article on the RSVP Club in Manhattan had led me to Mabel Mercer six years before. Arnie and I shared most of the Club's organization.

Arthur Wirtz, amazed by our ability to fill his stadium, came up with an offer. "If you could do that, with the stadium," Wirtz said, "you might take a look at some empty premises of mine on Walton Street, a club called the Colony."

I sensed that Wirtz, a huge man weighing 300 pounds, was offering me a real turkey. When I first saw the place, no doubt remained. The Colony Club had failed under four successive managements.

Still, I figured that if it had been a thriving concern it would never have been available to us. What had failed without the backing of *Playboy* magazine might do a sight better with it. I agreed to take it if the price was right.

Arthur Wirtz was not a multi-millionaire by chance. "You take the Colony," he told me, "and I'll let you have it rent-free, on a percentage lease. That means you get it for nothing if it takes in nothing. I only stand in for a small percentage of the gross."

"Only!" I doubt if even he realized at the time that he was on to one of the best little deals he was ever likely to make. The Club would bring him a small fortune.

I had hired an assistant, Don Gold, who later became editor of *Downbeat* magazine. Don and I estimated that Wirtz's share of that enterprise topped well over a million dollars in the first six years.

It also did *me* no harm. I was vice president of the company Hefner had set up to operate the Club and I owned a quarter of the shares. Arnie Morton owned another quarter. And Hefner and *Playboy* magazine had the rest.

Now the only problem was to find exactly the right staff, entertainment, equipment, décor, restaurant and cabaret facilities for our premises. And to steer well clear of any licensing pitfalls.

Chapter Three

BUNNIES FOR BREAKFAST

The bunny girl motif came later—initially from a girl I was dating named Ilse Taurins. We happened just then to be chewing over a mass of problems associated with a television series we called *Playboy's Penthouse*. Hefner was host and I was associate producer. The Club concept ran in tandem with this, so that discussions about one frequently drifted over into the other.

In this way the idea of feminizing the bunny symbol—which in the magazine was strictly male, with black bowtie—was born.

Ilse was appearing on our TV show, and she was quite often around while these talks were going on. She was a very beautiful young lady, a Latvian refugee with that strange Nordic bone structure and easy grace.

Both Hef and I enjoyed her company. She sometimes came up with bright notions. When she heard us talking about the waitresses for the proposed Club, she heard Hef say he fancied dressing them in "shortie nighties of some frilly material" and he wanted to call the waitresses "Playmates," after the magazine's centerfolds.

"Surely, whatever they wear, ought to be more serviceable than that," she said. "Why not give them a really individual look— linking them more to the magazine? Why not dress them as rabbits?"

Hefner chuckled. "I've thought about this, but the bunny in *Playboy* is male," he countered. "Well, the idea of girl bunnies may have possibilities, but I'd like to see it first. After all, when you consider how female rabbits mate with male rabbits, well ... it's certainly a sexy notion!"

Ilse's mother was a seamstress and Ilse persuaded her to produce a rough of the first bunny costume. I thought it was a letdown when I saw it. It looked more like a bathing costume with ears than an attractive garment for a cocktail waitress. I had a hunch Hef would discard the whole idea.

But not at all. After he had watched Ilse move about in her mother's sample costume for a while, he nodded thoughtfully." I like the tail," he said. "And the whole costume fits neatly into the Playboy concept. But what if we don't find enough girls with long legs to show it off?"

He walked over to Ilse and asked her to hike up the sides of her bunny costume, showing the fishnet stockings underneath and extending the length of her legs almost theatrically. The effect was astonishing. Once again, Hef had seen in a matter of seconds what others might never have seen.

Before the opening of the Chicago Club we arranged for the finished version of the bunny costume to be made and fitted to the first girls hired to wear it. They looked great.

Later, at Hef's suggestion, collar and cuffs—and the Playboy symbol, the black bowtie—were added. Hef felt that without some added decoration the costumes did, indeed, look too much like bathing suits.

The whole concept seemed so excitingly different in those days before the Club opened that I found myself wondering if it could ever be as popular with the public as it was with us. On opening night some of the bunnies found the costume uncomfortable. "These ears are killing us. We *all* agree they are impossible," one of them told me. I looked around and saw that several of the bunnies had already removed their ears. An opening night revolution was in the air.

I announced that all bunnies *must* wear their ears while working. "Impossible?" I guess not. We received no further complaint during the next twenty-one years that I was associated with the company.

We opened Leap Year night, 29 February 1960. With hindsight, its easy to see why the Club was so successful. Through the magazine we had proclaimed the novel idea of a place of entertainment and pleasure, with charming, attractive girls in attendance, but free of the lewdness which was easily found in Chicago nightlife at that time. Chicago was notorious for its strip joints; many little nightclubs and taverns offered "B-girls" who were thinly disguised prostitutes.

Like some of those that I encountered in London later on (clubs like the Georgian Pussy Club which advertised that it closed at midnight—to allow more time for the customers and the girls to get together), these were sexually and erotically explicit in their attractions. We were not, but we were still able to suggest a risqué and acceptably frisky atmosphere.

The first few months we did not even offer a cabaret. The Club was sophisticated—what we'd call "cool" and "laid back" today. The girls we employed as bunnies were straightforward, decent girls from nice families. Sure, they were pretty and the costume made them alluring to the eye. But the rules had been drilled into them. Any girl who slipped up was out. Because we were also *Playboy* magazine we had to bend over backwards to avoid anything that suggested we were going beyond the bounds of good taste.

Our bunnies had to be untouchable. That was why we made it an absolute decree—no telephone numbers to be given to members. As with the magazine, which linked an eye-catching ambience with solid, civilized reading matter, the Club rose above any suggestion of sex-for-sale. On its five floors we had a variety of luxuriously appointed rooms. In each of them, indeed in all of them, a member could take his wife, or a lady member her husband, without embarrassment.

The first live entertainment in the Club was a trio which played background music in the Club's "Living-Room"—one of several rooms which had been made to look as much like a bachelor flat as possible. It had coffee tables, low chairs and warm lighting. Originally we had decided against having performers in cabaret, but I was dedicated to the idea of some form of live entertainment and I may have been responsible for the change. Most probably I was still influenced by the powerful experience of listening to Mabel Mercer in New York and of bringing her to Chicago.

In spite of the fact that we spent very little on those early performers, and none of them was famous, I guess I was right. The feedback we got from members showed that live entertainment was very much what was wanted. In the end, I told Hef that we should consider stepping up that side of the Club's attractions, and he agreed.

Based on the principle we had evolved of presenting new talent, perhaps three acts at a time, I hired Mabel Mercer (my immortal aphrodisiac) to head our first major cabaret presentation. We had no great stage or lighting facility for her. I put her on in another of the Club's rooms we called "The Library," with the audience sitting around on cushions and Mabel in her chair, as always. I'm afraid she wasn't a big hit with our Playboy audience. After that, while Arnie Morton refined and polished the restaurant and bar side of the business, I went in continuous search of new talent.

We were soon established in a way we had never intended—as a cabaret club presenting the best new acts available.

That first night, queues formed outside the old Colony, now the Playboy Club. It was freshly decorated, and easily identifiable by the *Playboy* rabbit trademark embossed on a brass plaque alongside the entrance. Many of those waiting for the doors to open had already obtained their keys from us by mail, but many more were hoping to buy a key at the door. We had stressed in all our promotion that, after the payment of the initial $25.00 "key" membership, the Club offered *everything* at a set price of $1.50—drinks, cigarettes and meals.

Success was immediate. We didn't need to touch the loan facilities we'd arranged to cover anticipated launch costs. A flood of applications for membership arrived with every mail. The Club was set to make a mountain of money.

Chicago had never seen anything like it. Arnold Morton hired chefs and prepared menus which made a visit to the Club a delicious treat. Arnie's father was running a restaurant on South Shore Drive where Arnie had had his training. I had known them both when I was at the university. The place was very popular with students. It was a great hang-out. One of the first things I did when I joined *Playboy* was to pay them a visit in search of an ad for the magazine. By then they had moved to the lake-front.

I'll never forget that call. Old Man Morton C. Morton was an impressive-looking character with a large handle-bar moustache. "I'll take an advertisement with your magazine if you can think up a good idea, young man," he told me.

That night I told Hef, "Let me take a photographer over to Morton's place, and I think we'll book him on a series." In those early days, this was a good prospect.

My idea was to have a picture of Morton taken with an enormous, oversized cocktail glass and the slogan "I am Morton C. Morton, and I invented the Mortini. . . ." Then there was a spoof description of how to make it. "You take a gallon of gin . . ." and so on. I thought it made an amusing idea which would attract people to the restaurant.

I wrote the copy and Hef assigned the photographer. Old Man Morton was delighted. He ran the ad with us for quite a while. So, when we were planning the Club and realized that neither Hefner nor I had any experience in catering or running a first-class restaurant, I suggested Old Man Morton's son, Arnold. Fortunately, he was looking for just such an opportunity and was only too happy to join us from the very beginning and help with the whole catering plan. Later, as I had a hunch he would, Arnie became one of the most trusted and valued members of our team.

By now I'd made it clear to Hefner that I was going to make Playboy (the whole business, not just the magazine) my career. But if I was going to stay in the job, which meant staking everything on the enterprise I wanted to buy some of his shares. These had been issued at $1.00 each. Hef agreed that I could have 3,250 of them in all, which left him holding an all-powerful 68 percent stake. He retains his 68 percent today.

The shares were the best investment I ever made. Over the years they were split time and time again so that when Playboy Enterprises went public in 1971 my 3,250 shares had become 195,000 each quoted at $23.50. My holding had a net worth of $4,582,500. I was the second largest shareholder in the corporation.

I didn't sell any then, but a writer named Burt Zollo did. He had contributed a single article to one of Hef's first issues and been rewarded with a few shares in the magazine. These brought $2,350,000 when Playboy went public—easily the highest figure ever paid for a magazine article.

Hef had tried many times to buy the stock back from Zollo and it must have pained him to look back on that early deal when he gave low-valued stock in place of money.

The night we opened in Chicago we all seemed to sense that the future would exceed a lot of our expectations. I was already making more money than I ever had. Sales of *Playboy* were rising rapidly, attracting more advertising and gaining prominence on the news-stands—even those previously reluctant to handle us. Hef and I agreed that the next thing we had to do was start more clubs in *other* cities before our best ideas got "borrowed" by competitors. We even managed to get the bunny costume patented so it couldn't be ripped off legally.

There were discussions and planning sessions late into the night. Hefner agreed that we should move fast into new sites and cities. We planned schemes under which other operators could use our style and presentation in return for payment, and franchised clubs were already open in New Orleans and Miami, both of which were later purchased by Playboy. One of our management team, Tony Roma, was busy setting up a Playboy Club in Phoenix, Arizona. Then, to spearhead our nationwide expansion, I flew east to find us a site in the Big Apple—New York City.

In spite of the pressure of work in covering Manhattan real estate agents and going into all the pros and cons of the city's nightlife, I now had the chance to renew some very warm and pleasant acquaintanceships. By day I searched and scoured for premises, staff, decorators, builders—and for girls pretty enough and capable enough to be bunnies. At night, I made sure I didn't waste my time. I rarely got to bed before the early hours and almost never alone.

Whatever else, that Manhattan marathon of hard work by day and hard play by night proved that my constitution could take an awful lot of punishment ... and pleasure. And eventually I located premises which, after an expensive face-lift, would be ideal. They were on the same block as the Sherry Netherland Hotel.

At the same time I was scouting talent for Chicago. I needed artists who could hold the attention of a lusty crowd busy with food, drink and the bunnies. Higher-paid stars asked fees which outran our still slender budget.

So I had to snoop around. Looking back, it's surprising what turned up. A young singer named Barbra Streisand was mentioned to me, and I went to see her at a club in Greenwich Village. Terrific personality, great talent, but I didn't care much for her looks. I even had the temerity to suggest to her manager that Miss Streisand ought to consider having a nose job. My suggestion was fortunately ignored.

Nevertheless, Miss Streisand's demands seemed reasonable and there was no doubt about her quality as a performer. I offered her a contract at $350 a week to appear in Chicago for a three-week run, four shows a night, seven nights a week. In addition there was Playboy's standard option—five more three-week stints at the same money.

She accepted with what I perceived to be pleasure. We signed, and she seemed all set to go on when her new manager, my friend

Marty Erlichman, called to break off the engagement—because Barbra had got the chance to play in a musical on Broadway, "I Can Get It for You Wholesale." He agreed to settle under the terms of the American Guild of Variety Artists' ruling, by which an artist may either "pay or play." She would "buy out" her contract with us.

We never collected. And years later, when Streisand was in London to promote her movie, *Funny Girl,* I bumped into her at a party. I reminded her—half jokingly—that she still owed us those eighteen weeks. She shrieked and then turned her back on me as if I'd served her with a writ—which perhaps says more about the star system (and what it does to some people) than it does about this very talented artist.

I was not always so unlucky. I'm sure that Dick Gregory, one of America's top comedians, will never turn his back on Playboy. When I booked him to appear in our cabaret, he was working as a carwash attendant. The spot he filled for us was the start of his climb to fame and fortune.

Hef uncharacteristically left most of the floor show arrangements to me. He also entrusted Arnie Morton, Bob Preuss and me with setting up the New York Club. "I'll handle the magazine," he told me during one of our many planning sessions. "You three are better at getting these shows on the road."

Hefner's approach to dress, emphasized by wearing seldom more than a buttoned-up cardigan, slacks, and an open-necked shirt, gave an impression of casualness which belied his firm control of every aspect of his organization. This is true today when the press generally shows him wearing jump suits or bathrobes.

At that time I saw Hefner as a man who would not bend to the prevailing wind but would stand loyally behind the ideas and individuals he had faith in and would familiarize himself with every operational detail where there was any difference of opinion. I was proud to be involved with him in all Playboy ventures.

And in New York I was happy ultimately to be part of the team that presented him with a Club which in every way lived up to the image we had created in Chicago.

Hef had been divorced in the late fifties around the same time as I had. He began writing his philosophy, the ideals embodied in his magazine, at that time. It had led him away from the casual period a few years back when we used to hang around at bars and carry a stack of new issues of *Playboy* magazine, just off the press, to give to our favorite bartenders. By now Hef was moving into his reclusive shell, no longer the free-wheeling night owl.

He found the mansion home he was to make the Playboy empire's nerve center, at 1340 North State Parkway, Chicago. The house I helped him pick out belonged to the Isham family, partners with Robert Todd Lincoln in the law firm of Lincoln, Isham and Jones. When he added on the house next door he was able to offer visitors the added recreation of a full-scale bowling alley, with an automatic pin spotter. He no longer needed to venture outside for his entertainment.

For myself, these were years of such satisfying and creative development that looking back on them they seem to merge into one happy filmstrip. I was busy, and so busy enjoying myself when work ceased that sleep, rest, and sometimes even exercise took second place. Arnie Morton summed it up when he and I were discussing the menus for the Clubs one day. I'd been critical about his decision to put on more cold items and take off some of the hot dishes.

Getting excited as I often did in my younger days I cried, "But Arnie, why change a winning menu?" Arnie Morton looked at me with a sly, humorous glint in his eye. "Menu?" he said dryly. "The only menu you're interested in, Victor, is bunnies for breakfast!"

A good joke, perhaps, but a twist of the truth. In our position we had to guard against any suggestion that we might take some unfair advantage of the bunny waitresses. Whenever I dated a bunny it was generally through meeting her outside socially, or through mutual friends. You could say that, in a manner of speaking, I never—well, hardly ever—made passes at girls who carry glasses . . . at least, not while they were carrying them.

As I mentioned before, in the early days of the Playboy Clubs, we made a rule that the bunnies were not to give out their names and phone numbers, date customers, or go out with other staff members.

But we certainly didn't want them to feel that they couldn't go out with us! By "us" I mean the senior executives who were not in daily direct line of contact with the girls, but who managed the company; in particular, Hefner, Morton and myself. At the same time we didn't want the girls to feel coerced or harassed into dates. The bunnies had every right to refuse to go out with us.

Only once was my patience sorely tested. I had asked a bunny—a very pretty girl indeed—if she'd care to go out with me. She agreed. I then went to the trouble of getting theatre tickets and making a dinner reservation for after the show.

When I arrived at her apratment to pick her up, she announced with unprovoked hostility that she'd "changed her mind" and didn't want to go out with me. She offered no explanation.

I was furious. In my rage, I phoned the bunny mother and said that we didn't need *that* bunny anymore. I wanted her fired. She had broken her word, stuck me with a pair of theatre tickets and bruised my ego.

The bunny mother expressed reservations. She said that she didn't think it was in keeping with our policies that we should fire a girl for having broken a date. I didn't want to listen. I insisted on the bunny's dismissal.

The bunny mother called Hefner on the matter, and Hefner called me on the mat. He made me see that I was violating the principle that we ourselves had established. The fact that theatre tickets went to waste in this instance made it no more or less than the kind of rejection we might get if any girl stood us up.

Hef reminded me that we must be true to our policy of not in any way using the business relationship to punish the bunny.

The girl resigned a few weeks later of her own accord.

I recognized, of course, that Hefner was absolutely right in his reasoning. As the years went by, we became ever more and more careful to insure that a girl would at no time feel that her social life was something over which we had any control.

I should mention here the rumor that persisted for several years about "Playboy #1" cardholders. Gossip had it that the holders of "#1 Playboy" cards could have their pick of the bunnies in a seeming master-slave relationship in which the girls had to acquiesce. This obviously was pure fantasy. Had such a system or anything remotely like it existed, certainly a young lady somewhere would have said by now, "They made me sleep with them!" No such accusations or scandal has ever surfaced anywhere—and this is thousands and thousands of bunnies later.

I remember one incident when I'd been to bed with, not one, but two, girls. They were bunnies who worked in our Chicago club. The following day the shorter and younger of the two complained to her associates that I had "forced her" to have sex with me.

The story got back to Hefner, and he queried me about it. I said that in the first place there was never any question about this girl being willing to have sex. She'd actually agreed to go to bed with me and her friend, and in the second place I had the other girl as witness that I hadn't coerced the accuser.

Hefner stared at me thoughtfully. "Victor," he said, "I don't think it's going to improve your case to produce as a witness before a puritanical jury another girl who happened to be in bed with you at the same time."

I've always agreed with the maxim "Sex is like business; even when it's bad it's good." But it's the variety that has admittedly always appealed to me. The new conquest and the different experience are always the most exciting.

Thus it is something of a puzzle to me to see a picture in the newspaper of a miner, with his fat, ugly wife standing next to him, surrounded by his eighteen or nineteen children. I assume the chap must have an extremely strong libido. I don't see how it's possible that a man could continue going to bed with this lackluster lady and father all these children, when the wife so obviously lacks what I would consider to be—sex appeal.

On the other hand, I've been with hundreds of girls in the twenty-eight years since my divorce, and recognize that perhaps my promiscuity may conceal a form of impotence, an inability to be monogamous.

Why else constantly look for the stimulation of a new girl rather than sustaining an active sexual interest in a girl I've had many times. The too-familiar bed mate may draw wolf whistles from passers-by but if, as far as I'm concerned, she has lost her ability to be sexually exciting to me, so be it. I can think of several women I admire and respect who no longer interest me sexually but who would have the man in the street drooling.

We had a serious job to do. What had started off as a creative and exciting hayride had become big business. More and more people had come into the organization, enriching it with their own ideas and techniques. Indeed, I had begun to feel like Gulliver pinned down by a lot of tiresome restrictions and procedures. From what had been fun, my Playboy role had grown too close to that of Corporation Man. Would the next twenty years be a succession of gray flannel suits and conferences?

Also, I was finding it harder to keep in close contact with my friend, Hef. He was beginning to shut himself off from the world. Increasingly, he seemed to have faith in his own ideas alone and no one else's.

I consider myself capable of offering a few good ideas. It was frustrating to have to buck negative attitudes without being able to get through to Hef as I had in the past. Looking ahead it seemed to me that my future, if I stayed with Playboy, would become a treadmill of repetition and bureaucratic management.

My own keenness was causing friction in the firm—especially with Keith, Hef's brother. I decided I needed a break. I'd been with

Hef seven years. He was a sort of father figure to both Keith and myself, so that each of us was "competing for Dad's approval." I didn't see it that way at the time, but Hef told me himself a couple of years ago that he always felt the running competitiveness between me and Keith was like sibling rivalry between two brothers. It's certainly true we were the same age, two years younger than Hef, but even now I'm not convinced I ever saw Keith as a serious rival.

To me, Keith seemed to be on a different channel, more theatrical and less business-oriented. I had little to do with him. His job at first was as a room director in the Chicago Club, which we'd divided into a number of different rooms each with an individual theme. Later he became the official head of the Bunny Training Program. I think Keith invented the famous "Bunny Dip"—the stylized way of serving drinks that avoids any embarrassing bunny exposure.

It was my responsibility to check him at work from time to time, as I did everybody. My way, which I can see now was disconcerting, was to thrash problems out with the person responsible, rather than to write memos. I recall Keith was sometimes forgetful about switching on the electric signs I'd installed. These would flash on, announcing *Immediate Seating in the VIP Room* (or *The Penthouse* or *The Playroom*—or wherever we wanted to encourage more custom in any of the Club rooms).

Incidentally, we had to make a clear distinction between our keyholding members and members of a non-profit-making club, which in the United States all "clubs" have to be. So there was a problem over the use of our name "Playboy Club" which we avoided by calling our members "keyholders" and not, officially, "members." It was the late Paul Desmond, Dave Brubeck's magnificent alto sax player (and composer of "Take Five") who commented "beauty is in the eye of the keyholder," which seemed to me to sum it up very neatly.

Obviously the object of the signs was to increase our business and to give a service to our keyholders. When a manager like Keith failed to appreciate this and I observed that we were getting crowds in one room and none in others, I took the matter up with him. Other than that, I can't recall any trouble between us.

Keith and I were certainly worlds apart. My first sight of him was on a film of a children's TV program before he joined us at Playboy. He played a character named Johnny Jellybean and the kids loved him. Ours was not an enterprise for the under-sixteens, but Keith's charm still made him popular with both staff and customers.

Keith took it upon himself to report critically on the performers and shows I found for the Club. Once when I booked the soul-singing and piano-playing Aretha Franklin, he came to me with a worried look on his face. He knew I'd hired her for only $250 a week. He couldn't have been expected to predict her rise to stardom.

"She's no good, Victor," he told me. "She doesn't cut it. She's terrible. Why do you book acts like that?"

It all made me wonder if Keith wasn't too specialized for Playboy. Even so, I don't recall that he consciously affected my decision to leave. There were other considerations.

Actually it was Hef who precipitated my final decision to quit. He took me to task for having criticized one of the room directors, Joe Kastell. My continual interference in the day-to-day activities of the Club, he said, was disruptive. I was startled that a lowly room director could get me called on the carpet.

I had to face the fact that the promotional work I had put into building Playboy was no longer being recognized at true value. My suggestions were increasingly failing to get through. The $50,000 a year Hef was paying me was not the outer limits of my ambition. Now was the time, if ever, to make a move.

We talked it over and Hef said he understood my feelings. In some ways I think he felt I could be more useful offering him ideas for the Club and the magazine from the outside. He was also feeling his way towards a division of the two promotion departments, Clubs and magazine, both of which I headed. My departure would make it easy for him to hive off one from the other. Hef suggested I keep my ties with the company as a consultant. He'd pay me $75,000 a year and at the same time I'd be president of the still unopened New York Club, though on a non-executive basis. I had plans to start my own consulting and advertising firm and he offered to use my firm for public relations for the New York Club, too.

I felt like a poker player on a winning streak who'd shown his full house and was leaving the game a winner. My quarter share in the Clubs was going to be redeemable on my leaving the company. What had cost me very little cash (but a lot of hard work) was now valued at almost two million dollars. The temptations to cash this in were compelling. And I would still own the original shares in *Playboy* magazine which Hef had let me purchase for that hard-to-find $3,250. He wanted them back, but I held on.

It was finally arranged (with Bob Preuss negotiating the agreement) that I would be paid out for my shares over five years. This meant that I was seeing somewhere in the region of $400,000 a year, with work in hand for my own business. There was no difference of opinion about this. Hef and I remained friendly. After June 1962, when I left the company, I visited him often. But my work for Playboy was considerably reduced.

There was one piece of unfinished business. All our Clubs required liquor licenses in the various states and New York was no exception. The trouble was that application for the license had involved Playboy in a strange series of events.

In May 1960, Arnold Morton had a call from Ralph Berger, a talent agent in Chicago. Berger had heard that we were setting up in New York and offered to "put in a good word" with the New York State Liquor Authority chairman, seventy-three-year-old Martin Epstein. In a roundabout way, Berger let Morton know that it would cost Playboy "at least $50,000" to get the license.

Construction was moving ahead rapidly and about two million dollars of Playboy money was committed. Also, we'd announced the opening and cash for new memberships was pouring in. As in Chicago, we were expecting to see all of our costs back in the $25 keys fees even before the doors opened. Without a liquor license we were dead.

I had faith in Arnie Morton. This stemmed from the time when I had seen him operate his own place in the fifties. This was a private key club called the Walton Walk located on Chicago's near northside, not far from the Playboy offices. Arnie's management, and his way of getting what he wanted, convinced me that he could be relied on to overcome any problems in our path.

With Bob Preuss, we went to see Epstein. Outside, a man costumed in top hat, spats and tailcoat was walking up and down with a sign reading "The State Liquor Authority is crooked and corrupt." Presumably, he was a liquor store owner who had been put out of business by the extortion tactics we were about to face. By the time we came out again I felt like joining him.

Epstein was specific in his demand. Either we put the money across his desk in cash, or he would never allow us to operate in New York. We told him cash was out of the question, our business was not a cash business. "Okay," he said, "then what you do is you hire Judson Morhouse, and he bills you. He's a lawyer."

L. Judson Morhouse was more than a lawyer. He was also Chairman of the New York State Republican Party and a close advisor to Governor Nelson Rockefeller. If we paid the money to him for fake legal work our chances of exposing it as blatant extortion while Republican Rockefeller governed the State were paper-thin.

There was only one way, I suggested to Hefner on our return. "If we go to Frank Hogan, the New York District Attorney, and blow the whistle on Morhouse and Epstein, he's sure to take action, Hogan is a Democrat."

"Wait a minute, Lownes," Hefner said. "That's dangerous talk. We can't afford to bring the whole machinery of the State down on our necks before we even get to open the Club."

On Hefner's mind was the ease with which the licensing authorities could legitimately ban our application. Before a license could be issued to serve liquor in a club, any number of conditions had to be satisfied. For one thing the lighting should be sufficient to enable anyone to "read a newspaper"—and this applied to the whole of the premises. So if an inspector found a shaded place—say under a piano—where this was not possible, it could be the excuse for refusal. These petty-fogging conditions placed tremendous power in the hands of the issuing authorities and led to considerable corruption.

So, in Hef's opinion, and he may have been right, the risk was not worth taking. With so much political power backing the corrupt individuals, whom could we appeal to? We agreed we'd have to pay the $50,000 extortion to Epstein via Morhouse—but we'd make sure we never used his legal services in any way at all.

But we hadn't heard the last of Morhouse and his demands. We received word that he would appreciate a payment of $100,000, as well as an option to buy a further $100,000 worth of Playboy stock, and the right to open a chain of gift shops in all Playboy Clubs. We managed to duck this additional blackmail attempt. Then, after opening on December 15, 1962, Playboy filed a complaint with Hogan and a long, legal battle began, lasting two years. A grand jury heard the testimony of our executives and handed down a vote of thanks to Hefner's organization for having the courage to come forward and fight the extortion.

Even Governor Rockefeller thanked Hefner and his company, promising that the State would not retaliate. Frank Hogan, the Democratic New York DA, moved into action against Berger and Epstein. Berger was convicted—his telephone had been tapped when he put his demands to us—and sentenced to one year in prison. His conviction was ultimately overturned by the US Supreme Court on the grounds that the wire-tap had been illegal. Epstein's failing health and age prevented his being brought to trial. The scandal ended Morhouse's political career and, to Rockefeller's great embarrassment, the Chairman of the Republican Party in the State of New York was convicted and sentenced to serve a term of imprisonment. Governor Rockefeller commuted this on the grounds of Morhouse's ill-health.

Later we successfully fought the restrictions on cabaret licences against a number of puritanical and what appeared to us vindictive objections to our work in exposing the corruption in the SLA.

Helped by the advertising and mailing blitz launched through the magazine at that time, key sales of 60,000 had come in before the opening. The Club was off to a promising start.

I watched from the sidelines. Six months after my departure from Playboy, I had an office in my apartment in the St. Moritz Hotel in New York, with two girls on my staff. One of them, Barbara Harrison, later became a novelist, and her book, *The Pagans,* tells the thinly veiled story of a magazine like *Playboy*—with the heroine running off with a magazine executive who stands up to the bad guys. Maybe she meant to model this on me, but by that time Hef was the one handling that sort of problem without me.

Chapter Four
THE HUTCH ON THE PARK

I was really enjoying myself, spending most of my time in New York, seeing lots of theatre and dating a variety of gorgeous girls. I was still connected with Playboy and had free run of the Playboy Clubs which were springing up all over the United States. I can't claim that I concentrated much effort into my small advertising agency because I never really felt that I had left the Playboy organization. I kept thinking that before long I would find my way into something more strenuous and challenging and somehow it would connect with Hefner and Playboy.

Any spare time I had during the summer, I spent at a house I rented on Fire Island. The island is an unusual playground as well as a Federal bird sanctuary. Motor cars are forbidden except for a few beach taxis, and life is both leisured and entertaining. My rented house had been built by Michael Butler, the original producer of *Hair*. It was in the Talisman district and was later torn down to accommodate the bird sanctuary. But that summer it was high on the jet-set pecking order of smart resorts.

Among my neighbors were Ahmet Ertegun, son of a former Turkish Ambassador to the United States and President of Atlantic Records; Peter Beard, photographer and railroad fortune heir; and a notorious race-horse owner who made headlines when she accidentally shot her husband. All the houses were Japanese-type wooden structures with sliding panels looking out on the Atlantic Ocean, and I regularly filled mine with girls who were clamoring to get away from the sweltering Manhattan summer. As a result, I was considered quite the live-wire by the Talisman community.

I also had a number of celebrated visitors while I was there. Among them was Cy Coleman who wrote the Lucille Ball musical *Wildcat*—vehicle for that great standard "Hey, Look Me Over." His other shows included *Little Me, Barnum* and *On the Twentieth Century*. While I was with Hefner, I'd gone to Cy when I wanted a theme song for Playboy and he wrote us a great number which remains the Playboy theme to this day.

Anyone who has ever played a Playboy pinball machine would recognize the tune. Every time the ball drops into the Jacuzzi "Grotto" Section, a few bars of Cy's song heralds the achievement—though whether Cy gets a royalty payment I've never discovered. He certainly should. The machine, made under license by Bally, sold 25,000, three times as many as their standard models. It's sort of a house rule at Playboy that whenever Hefner appears on television, Cy's theme song is played in the same way that "Hail to the Chief" greets any ceremonial appearance of the president.

Hefner is probably the only major publisher in history who has made himself recognizable to millions. Few would recognize Rupert Murdoch. Would anybody have recognized William Randolph Hearst or Henry Luce? Hef, with his pipe, is instantly known to almost everyone who has heard of *Playboy*. The magazine has benefited enormously from this personal publicity.

This hype began back in 1959 and the early sixties when Hef produced and hosted his own television shows, *Playboy's Penthouse,* later called *Playboy after Dark*. These were variety-style programs with a house-party atmosphere: Hef greeted his often dinner-jacketed guests and introduced the performers to the viewers at home. As associate producer, I also occasionally took part, in the background. I saw how professionally he projected his personal charisma. If they lost a little money for *Playboy,* the fact that these programs were syndicated throughout the United States gave the magazine publicity others couldn't equal. The benefits spread to the magazine and everything else connected with *Playboy* and its creator.

It's something of an irony that Hef, who likes nothing better than to stay inside his mansion among his personal friends and his built-in pleasures, has established this recognizable public image. Later, when he moved his base from Chicago to Los Angeles, the uniqueness of his reclusive life in Chicago largely disappeared. The Hollywood community includes many who are absolute hermits compared to Hefner. So although he identifies with the superstars and regularly entertains people like Jack Nicholson, Warren Beatty, Tony Curtis, Ryan O'Neal and others, the move to LA has cost him a part of his individuality.

It's a fact that Hefner seldom leaves his own living-room, screening-room, jacuzzi, bedroom apartment-office, or garden-cottage games-room; and is surrounded by bodyguards (against some of the kooky characters who send him hate-mail and threaten his life). Yet an invitation to be a guest on a major television show—the popular *Johnny Carson Show* or similar mass-audience events—will generally get a favorable response from him. That in itself seems to me to illustrate an eagerness to maintain his public image in spite of a rather justifiable sense of paranoia.

Travelling holds little interest for him. When he got his own DC-9 jet plane, the "Big Bunny," he used it mainly to zoom back and forth to LA to hold hasty business meetings in the Chicago mansion. With air-conditioned limousines always on the tarmac to sweep him off to his destination, there wasn't much difference in his being in one place or the other.

Getting back to my own position, I was gathering my strength for another bite at the commercial world—and becoming very interested indeed in travelling, especially abroad. I wanted to see Europe and other countries which, unlike Hefner, I had never seen. He'd invited me to go to France with him in 1958 for the Cannes Film Festival, but I'd been too busy with work on the magazine and had had to pass up the opportunity. Now I wanted to move on; New York and Talisman were beginning to lose their attractions.

It struck me one night when I was standing on the terrace of my New York apartment overlooking Central Park. The girl spending the evening with me was a real New Yorker. I doubt if she shared the wonder I felt at the strange contrast between that view of the Park— beautiful against the New York skyline— and what I knew to be its menace.

"Odd, isn't it?" I mused. "Just to think that with all that beauty nobody can walk through there after dark."

"I did," she said.

"And what happened?"

"I was raped."

Suddenly, it was very cold out there. Maybe I'd had enough of this two-faced city for a while. The warmth Playboy gave me had dropped several degrees the moment I officially left the organization. Towards the end of 1963, my independent journey was becoming less attractive. I felt a strong urge to get back into the Playboy operation in a real sense, to give a meaning to my working life which the consultantcy and the non-executive presidency of the New York Club couldn't possibly provide.

Bob Preuss had been in touch with me more than once. Hef still wanted to buy out my shares in the magazine. These were not worth a great deal more than the $3,250 I had paid for them. At the time I left him, Hef had made me an offer of $25,000, but I'd told him: "First, finish off buying my shares in the Club, then we'll talk about it." I now knew that I didn't want to sell out, I wanted to get back in.

Playboy had much more to offer me. I went to Hefner and told him I wanted to return. I added that what I really wanted was to go to Europe for him. I knew he was considering setting up Playboy Clubs outside the States.

He was receptive to my plan. "I'll go to London, look around, and see if it's possible to set up our operation profitably," I told him. At that time I had no idea that gaming would become a part of the enterprise.

The arrangement we made was probably overgenerous on my part, but I was looking to the future. Since I was being paid for my share in the Clubs over the years, I had no great personal need. I agreed to take $50,000 a year without expenses or budget to set up if I did find conditions suitable for us in England.

In the beginning I would work in my living quarters in London. Later, with financial director Bob Preuss, I was to work out fairer financial arrangements. As always in the company, these were budgeted in terms of the initial investment. And, of course, my future terms would depend upon my success.

Taking my two children with me, I flew to England on 27 December 1963—a date suggested by my tax advisers so that I could be resident outside the United States for the full year beginning 1 January. The kids were out of school for the Christmas holiday so it seemed a good idea to bring them with me. And I wanted Val, who would remain with me, to enjoy the best education England could offer.

I'd entered him for Stowe School, David Niven's alma mater. It was just outside Buckingham, and is one of England's younger public schools. Later Val moved to Millfield in Somerset which has considerably more advanced teaching methods and—the part Val liked—Millfield is coeducational. For a while we toured around Europe, visiting Paris, Rome and other cities and had our fill of the culture scene. Then I got down to work.

Three months after I arrived in London I took a three-year lease on a house at No. 3 Montpelier Square in Knightsbridge. The rent was 75 guineas a week, about $180.00. When my lease ran out the house sold for $75,000 and I could have bought it for that but didn't, to my great loss. Recently it changed hands for the equivalent of one million dollars.

The house was an ideal residence for the head of the Playboy operation in Britain, and over the next few years many of the world's jet-setters came to share that opinion. To begin with, I was anxious to settle where we were going to be. Could I find the right setting for a London Playboy Club? And how would British bunnies stack up against their American counterparts—in every sense of the word!

For the first six months I chased around to every real estate office in town. I must have walked over miles of vacant properties in Mayfair and the West End. But the bunny problem was no problem at all. It took no time for me to recognize that British girls were at least as lovely and capable as their US counterparts.

Tony Roma was working for me, and together we hand-picked the first six girls. These were to spearhead the operation. I planned to use them as a public relations team after they had spent six months training in Chicago. Ordinarily I left the selection of bunnies to the Club staff, but it was important that these girls should be especially good in every way, in order to get the Club off to a running start. So I was personally involved in selecting them.

They were stunningly beautiful. One in particular appealed to me. Dolly Read came from Bristol. At first sight of her, Tony wanted to veto her as a selection on the grounds that she was a little too plump. I refused to accept his criticism and as things turned out I am very glad I did.

Dolly had been the girlfriend of pop-singer Adam Faith. She had a fascination for entertainers, especially comedians. She had a great sense of humor and a marvellous laugh. As Dolly and I became friendly I enjoyed the way she roared with laughter at any witty remark or joke, and always seemed to be in the best of spirits.

Dolly didn't amuse all the men in her life after she left me. She took up with Trini Lopez, the orchestra leader, who was in Britain as an actor making a film, *The Dirty Dozen*. I understand that Lopez grew very jealous of Dolly, and she left him, to escape the prison of his jealousy. I wasn't surprised to hear that she then moved on to a close friendship with comedian Tommy Smothers.

She was the best audience any stand-up comic could wish for—as Dick Martin, one of the famed TV *Laugh-In* hosts, realized when, after she moved to the US, he frequently dated her. In the end Dick Martin was the one who decided she was too good an audience to lose, and married her.

When I saw Dolly again she had spent some time in the States, and Hefner was so charmed by her that he selected her to be an English Playmate. She was staying at his Chicago mansion with the other English bunnies. I was a little disappointed to see that my plump and cuddly girl from Bristol—with those beautiful "Bristols"—had dieted down to Hollywood proportions. What a waste of all that talent, I thought!

The Montpelier Square house had five bedrooms, usually occupied by visiting friends from the States. Occasionally I put up some of the candidate bunnies in need of somewhere to stay in London. There was a magnificent dining-room built into the garden and designed to look like an oriental greenhouse. The focal point of the house was my study, a nice big room filled with soft leather couches and with a bar at one end. At the other end, I placed my desk right under the front window so that friends driving by could see whether I was in or not.

That house was perfect for entertaining, at a time when all London was swinging. As the man behind the London Playboy I had a big edge. Stars and celebrities—the Beatles, Telly Savalas, Laurence Harvey, Woody Allen, Judy Garland and a galaxy of others—visited me at my house at different times and on different occasions.

And, of course, my men friends included some of the world's most adventurous lady-killers and sought-after matinée idols.

One day I put their reputations to the test. I applied to a computer dating firm. They sent me a whole list of girls' telephone numbers. Each of these girls, I was told, was ready and willing to be called by a man she'd never met and asked out for a date. One Sunday afternoon, when Michael Caine, Terence Stamp and Warren Beatty were sitting around in my living room, I got out the phone numbers, explained where they'd come from, and made a bet with my friends.

"Five pounds (ten dollars) of my money says that you won't be able to make a date with any of these girls," I wagered. "Only one condition—none of you must use any other name than your stage name."

I guess they didn't realize what I was very sure about: that no ordinary English girl would believe, for one moment, that she was actually being called up by a universal heart-throb who had her number from a dating service.

Michael Caine picked up the telephone. I do believe he thought he was on to a good thing. The girl he called first was named Sue. "Hello, Sue," he said in his best stage-Romeo voice. "This is Michael Caine. Yes, that's right, the actor. I understand from Computer Dating that you might be available to go out with me one evening this week ..."

Michael's face as the line went dead was something I'll never forget. Before it did, I'd heard a sharp burst of laughter at the other end, and so had he. Warren Beatty laughed as loudly as anybody, but he was the next to try.

I'll spare my friends' embarrassment over the rest of that afternoon's performance, except to say that I won my bet with all of them. Not one of our sexy-voiced superstars managed to convince those unlucky girls that they were not imposters. And things got even worse when Michael Caine started asking Warren Beatty to get on the phone to assure the young lady he wasn't a fake!

The real kicker came when I was able to let them know next day how I had fared—using my own less notorious name. I actually called up all three girls that afternoon and made dates with each one of them.

At the time I was enjoying more than my fair share of romance. The exotic Latin American beauty, Viviane Ventura, was seventeen when I met her and just breaking into films. She had long, jet black hair, huge gobstopper eyes, and a curvy little body that made it difficult for any man to resist. There was just one problem. Viviane was a virgin.

Though she was more than willing to lose her virginity to me— and I found it very difficult to turn her down—I figured that if I became Viviane's first lover she might well get hung up on me. I decided I could live without that. I was seeing a lot of leggy blonde actress Joanna Pettet. And although I have never had any objections to dating more than one girl at a time, I can only cope with one heavy emotional involvement at a time.

None of this deterred Viviane in the slightest. She had set her mind on going to bed with me, and if all that stood in the way was her virginity then she would solve that problem.

Help came for her in the person of actor Stuart Whitman. Stu was in London playing the lead in *Those Magnificent Men in Their Flying Machines*. And he was living just around the corner from me.

I don't know what kind of deal Viviane made with Stu, but one morning bright and early she came banging on my front door. "I've taken care of my little problem," she announced proudly. "I hope it makes you happy to know you're not my first lover." It seems that good neighbor Stu Whitman broke the ice, as it were.

How could I argue with her after that? My romance with Viviane lasted about two years, but although she came close to being a central figure in my life she never really dominated my scene. I always made sure things didn't get too serious. And there was one occasion when I was glad about that.

One night, when I least expected it, I received a visit from Viviane's mother, Barbara. Viviane was missing and Barbara was convinced she was with me. I think Barbara must have been a little frightened of me, for instead of coming to my house alone she arrived with a friend of hers named Bonita.

I invited both women into my study, fixed them a drink and assured Barbara Ventura that her daughter was absolutely not on the premises.

Barbara didn't believe a word I said. "I'm sure you have her hidden somewhere in this house," she declared.

If you really believe that," I said, becoming irritated, "search the house. Then you'll see that she isn't here."

"I'm not going upstairs in this house," she protested. "You never know what's going on here."

Then she turned to her friend. "Bonita," she said, "you search the house."

Dutifully I took Bonita on a tour of 3 Montpelier Square. With a great deal of attention to detail I showed her all the top-floor bedrooms. To demonstrate that I had nothing to hide, I escorted Bonita to my own bedroom on the second floor. There was no Viviane, no girls; nothing was going on. Then Bonita took a hand in events. Bonita was one cool lady. When we finally came downstairs and into the study she turned to Barbara Ventura and said: "I can absolutely assure you that not only is Viviane not here, but she hasn't been here for at least two hours ..." Now that's what I call good detective work.

After Viviane and I split up, we remained close friends and continue so to this day. I attended her wedding to Frank Duggan, a property developer, and it was Frank who helped me to find No. 1 Connaught Square, where I lived from 1967 to 1974. Now they're divorced and are both still good friends of mine.

My first few days in London I'd stayed at the Hilton Hotel—ever loyal to my old friend Nicky Hilton. There'd been something in the newspaper columns about my coming over to open up the Club. The real estate people came on to me in a big way. One of the guys visited my room in the hotel, pointed across at the Park Lane building which later became the Playboy Club and tried to sell me on it.

"That's the building for you, Mr. Lownes, right there," he enthused. "It's only just been completed and we haven't sold any part of it yet. You can take your pick." Actually, I soon found that they had already closed a deal on one of the flats. It had gone to the notorious washing-machine tycoon, John Bloom. That put me off at the time.

"It's too small for a club," I told the agent. "Let me know when you have something larger."

Then Bloom went broke, and I realized that his flat on the fourth floor could now probably become part of the Club. On that basis, I agreed to sign a sixty-three-year lease on the building.

So we had our building. The rent was $160,000 a year, with the usual stinger in the tail of the contract—rent reviews after the first fourteen and then every twenty-one years after that. On the first of these, in 1981, the rent went up to $900,000 a year. Bob Preuss is no longer with Playboy but he should remember that way back in 1967 we could have bought the building for a million.

My assistant Tony Roma just arrived from Chicago to help me and he brought his new wife, a singer named Bonnie Jacobs. They had a baby in London but it was born with a club foot and a cleft palate— both, thanks to modern surgery, corrected. Nevertheless, Tony was very upset and he convinced himself that the child's deficiencies were somehow due to English water and food. He was in such a state about it that I felt I had to let him go back to America. He left me to go to Montreal and open up a Playboy Club there.

I was sorry to lose Tony, but in some ways I thought at the time it was a good thing. Playboy had always managed to steer clear of any kind of association with the shady characters who'd made their presence known to us in Chicago. Nevertheless, word reached me that Tony's first wife, whom he left to marry Bonnie Jacobs, had connections with an organized crime family. There was always the faint possibility that Tony's former in-laws might resent his having left his first wife and come after him, then perhaps try to muscle in on our business.

I didn't really fall for this paranoid concept, but the whispers were around. I absolutely knew Tony had nothing whatever to do with any such rubbish. I had to let him go. He remains a good friend of mine to this day. Indeed, after I was fired, he gallantly called to tell me that I could count on him for a half-million dollar investment in any new project I went into. His Tony Roma rib restaurants are a sensational success.

Morton was sending over more and more people to help me as the opening date, June 1966, approached. He himself flew over for six months, bringing his family. And the distinguished artist and *Playboy* illustrator Leroy Neiman also came over to paint pictures for the Club.

We gave Leroy a studio at 45 Park Lane for the work. I was in there one day, fast asleep from exhaustion, when he found me. Leroy drew a picture of me in that condition which hangs on my wall at Stocks. He entitled it "Vic at His Best."

Another new helper was Henry Goldsmith, whom I recently hired to build the Playboy complex in Atlantic City, New Jersey. A cigar-smoking, likeable guy, Henry somehow upset a few people from the Chicago office and I was pressured into getting rid of him soon after the opening. He is now running his own business in the Boston area.

Finally there were Matt Metzger, an early Playboy administrator who has since died, and Hefner's buddy John Dante, who recently started his own highly successful club in Los Angeles called "Touch."

While all this was going on, I not only had very little time to party but, as managing director of the Club, I had to keep clear of any scandal. Inside the Club it was equally important for me to keep a distance between myself and the many beautiful girls I employed. If and when I wanted to date one of them, I had to be discreet about it. My invitation would invariably be through my secretary, or the bunny mother, and I only asked out bunnies whom I had also met socially outside the Club.

One or two unpleasant little events had got into the press, but nothing serious. In 1962, the year Hefner and I parted active company, I had got involved in a brawl with an insulting guy in a Chicago nightclub, who sued me. The case never came to court, but I settled out of court by paying him $5,000.

Two years after that, while I was in London, an ex-bunny managed to make a convincing case for my being the father of her child. The first blood test report said I wasn't the father. The bottom line was that I made arrangements to support the child, a little girl. Before that happened we went through something of a legal marathon.

I certainly didn't deny the possibility, or that I'd had an affair with the mother. She was a very pretty red-head named Beverley Schoenfeldt, whom I had met on Fire Island while she was working as a bunny at the New York Club. She applied for a job as my chauffeur. Since no cars were allowed on the island, that was the last thing I needed her for—but we did spend a lot of enjoyable time together that summer of 1963. Indeed, Beverley did spend one particularly delightful weekend with me, and when she left I felt something had gone out of my life.

It had. A beautiful blue sweater was missing from my drawer. It was one I'd bought because it resembled one I'd seen in an Alain Delon movie.

I was angry about this. Later in the day I had to go down to Ocean Bay, another Fire Island community, to deal with a problem on my boat, and who should I see but my lovely weekend guest strolling with a man on the quay—a man remarkable only in that he was wearing my lovely blue sweater.

"Hey!" I shouted. "Hold it! That's my sweater!" Beverley and her friend began to walk faster and faster away from where I stood on the boat. In the end they were actually running. I decided that I had better things to do than chase a lady with such taking ways.

But weeks later, she telephoned me to report that she was pregnant. "What," I queried, "does that have to do with me?"

"You're the daddy," she told me. I hoped my chuckle didn't sound too heartless.

"What about the fellow you gave my sweater to?" I asked. Beverly's reply still astonishes me.

"Well, I am sorry about that," she said. "But if you really insist, I'll get it back."

Frankly, I'd more or less forgotten the whole incident by the time I got to London and became involved in the Club opening. Then one morning I opened the *Daily Express* and there, in the column reporting "Goings-on in America" was a headline, PLAYBOY'S EUROPEAN BOSS IN PATERNITY SUIT.

According to the *Express* columnist, I was going to have to pay $100 a week to my sweater-loving friend. Beverley had gone to court in New York and, since she was a Florida resident and I was a resident of England by then, my lawyers at first thought the whole thing lay outside the New York jurisdiction. We ignored it. But finally we did seek a hearing in New York.

I went to London's College of Forensic Medicine to have blood tests taken and mailed across to the American court. These, were the first reports that showed I wasn't the father of Beverley's child. But that didn't satisfy the New York State experts.

"Those people in London are always getting it ballsed up," their top man insisted. "We want those tests reviewed."

Accordingly, the stuff went back to the laboratory technicians and after another wait I was told I "could not be excluded" as the father. Meanwhile, my lawyers had managed to locate the guy with my blue sweater, and he had managed to convince everybody that *he* could not be the father.

I concluded that the only decent thing, for the baby's sake more than anyone else's, was to stand good for her future. I had a Trust Fund set up in the sum of $40,000 to see the little girl through until the age of eighteen. The lawyer's fee was $24,000. It was a $64,000 question I could have done without.

If it hadn't been for that damn sweater, I might have done more for Beverley than I did—even though I'm still not sure that the child is mine. The New York City case was heard before a referee, not a judge. Maybe he shared my view. When Beverley's lawyers started making a fuss over what I was offering for the child, he advised them to accept it: "Since I would never award you that much."

The child's name is Liza and she is now eighteen. Two years ago she called me up to say hello, and she sounded like a really nice person. I didn't go into details with her. I certainly didn't tell her that I had made a present to each of the two lawyers, Stanley Plesent and Howard Squadron who handled my case. They each received one of those blue sweaters.

I returned to London after that hearing, relieved, in a way, that the affair was settled and I could get on with my job. We were approaching the all-important opening of Europe's first Playboy Club and we had problems.

Only after I had arrived in England did I learn that cabaret owner Paul Raymond was using the bunny concept. On top of this he was publishing a magazine, *Men Only,* which was a copy of *Playboy.*

I went to his place in Soho, and saw his girls dressed almost exactly like our bunnies. My lawyers told me there was nothing we could do to stop him—in fact, he might even stop us from "copying" his motif in our Club!

I offered $4,000 to buy out the rights. He said $20,000. I went away and we never discussed it again. But his girls stopped wearing bunny costumes when we opened. It leaves me still wondering about the outcome if he'd persisted in using our design.

Another problem was a strip joint that called itself "The Soho Playboy Club." Not only did this operate in Soho but it actually used pictures from *Playboy* magazine as come-ons in its display-cases in front of the place.

Fortunately this back-street dive wasn't listed in the London telephone directory. Nevertheless, after my run-in with Raymond I didn't want lingering difficulties from this or any other source. I decided that any attempt by me to buy the name could lead to a lot of expense and trouble. It might even make them realize they had something from which they could make more money than they ever thought possible by demanding we buy them out. I ignored them, shut my eyes to their existence, crossed my fingers and opened *our* Playboy Club.

Oh, just one thing. On the off-chance that it might get some of our business by accident, the "Playboy" strip-joint in Soho started listing its phone number in the directory!

Chapter Five

WHEN THE CHIPS ARE DOWN

I had come to Britain intending to open a Playboy Club similar to the one in Chicago. I didn't know that England had just legalized gambling unintentionally with the passage of the 1960 Betting and Gaming Act—which was humorously nicknamed the Vicars' Charter because what it was supposed to do was legalize whist drives at church galas and functions of that nature. Some clever operators found that there was a definite loophole that enabled people to open casinos, providing they only offered games of equal chance. And by letting people take the bank for games that have an edge for the house, they felt they were all offering the same chance to each player.

In other words, if you felt up to it, you could agree to take the bank for five spins of the roulette wheel and so could every other player. Then you would all be playing against each other with the same chance and nothing favoring the house. The house depended on most people's unwillingness to risk taking the bank.

So gaming sprang up all over England and there was no regulating licensing law. There were thousands of people driving a coach and six horses through the 1960 Gaming Act by offering games of theoretical equal chance and operating casinos. There were more than a thousand places in Britain where casino games were in operation ... pubs with a single roulette layout or a blackjack table, clubs where a regular evening session of chemin-de-fer or baccarat became the thing.

Not only were they openly running gaming tables (some of which had been illegally in use in back rooms), but the 1960 Act had given birth to establishments where gaming of a fairly sophisticated sort took place throughout Britain. On advice, I visited Crockfords, one of London's most famous and reputable gaming clubs. I wanted a closer look.

The first thing I noticed was that every player taking part in the game of roulette had to be offered the opportunity of running the bank, in line with the Vicars' Charter. Though I am no great gambler, and my experience of Las Vegas and other American casinos had been limited to winning and losing a few dollars (including the night in Indiana with Nicky Hilton when I had actually walked away $23 richer), it seemed obvious that this was an opportunity in a million.

I asked for the bank every time I could. Running it, I found I was able to make a sizeable profit—and at the same time to gain a clear idea of the eagerness with which English men and women of means would be attracted to a spinning wheel or the turn of a card. That the British were a nation of gamblers had been told to me in my youth, but now I was seeing evidence of it night after night.

Why not gaming at the Playboy Club? I thought this was an opportunity for us to expand our full entertainment package by offering gaming along with our food, beverage, cabaret and bunnies. And my first thought was that I would invite Crockfords to run our casino operations for us, because we had no previous experience in that industry.

I negotiated with Tim Holland and Captain Alan Black who had given up their interest in Crockfords. The new ownership and administration was headed by an experienced industrialist, Dennis Poore. He seemed to be out of his element in the world of gaming. However, he agreed to my suggestion and we made a deal.

Crockfords would pay us $100,000 a year's rent for the use of our Park Lane premises as a casino. And we would receive half the net profits from the gaming. If that deal had gone through, Playboy would have made millions, but millions less than it eventually did. Worse still, when the 1968 Act came into force in 1970, it is doubtful if a management arrangement would have been legal. Crockfords by then had changed hands several times and was now owned by some dubious Corsican French operators. They were denied a license under the new act. That would have been our fate, too.

However, what happened in my negotiations is that Crockfords backed out at the last minute. The one good thing that emerged from this was that I hired their chief accountant, Mike Bassett, as our first casino manager.

Bassett was meticulous and especially good at training a staff. He received a percentage of our casino profits and if he'd stayed with us, would have become a multi-millionaire. But he was obsessed with the idea of owning a piece of the equity, and this we wouldn't give to him. Finally, he resigned to work for the Knightsbridge Sporting Club where the owners did give him a piece of the business.

Unfortunately for Bassett—and for British gaming—he found his new employers guilty of cutting corners in a way which he could not stomach. Much as I did, later on in other circumstances, Bassett went to the British Gaming Board and raised a great fuss. As a result he was fired, left gaming, and went into the insurance business where he has since been very successful. In many ways, his is a story paralleling my own, in that the hero became the villain-of-the-piece by standing up to the real villains.

So all connection with Crockfords ended. I received a curious reminder of our early dealings with them years later. In anticipation of their running our casino, Crockfords had ordered a large supply of chips from an American manufacturer. These had Playboy's rabbit head on them and were therefore of no use outside our casino. But, since Crockfords had made a down payment deposit of

$20,000, if I was to assume the contract, they'd get their money back. When I talked to the American manufacturer he tried to screw us out of the $20,000, so the deal fell through.

They had already made the chips. I had to get a completely new set in different colors from another manufacturer. And years later, someone tried to use Crockfords' Playboy chips in our casino. We traced them to a staff member at one of the top Nevada gaming casinos in Las Vegas, and we turned over all information to the authorities in Nevada. I don't know the end of the story.

Chips and plaques can have a special attraction for gamblers. We had a plaque made of solid gold costing £8,000 ($16,000) and carrying a face value of £100,000 ($200,000).The value was set in diamond chips. When gold went up in value, our £100,000 plaque rose to be actually worth £20,000. Even so, I really hoped somebody would walk off with it, leaving the hundred thousand they were entitled to receive in our cash desk.

When we ordered it from a London jeweller, I wasn't at all sure that such a valuable chip would be more than a high-priced piece of window dressing—something exciting to show the press. In fact it was used, many times. Business eventually made it necessary to put plastic, £100,000 plaques in circulation.

Our other plaques and chips were mainly plastic but I had the Franklin Mint make a bunnyhead chip in a silver-type alloy. These were valued at £1 ($2) and they disappeared regularly—which was fine with us, because they cost only 23 pence (45¢). I found that for another 10 pence I could get a keychain made to surround the chip and I offered this free, as an added incentive to walk off with them.

One weird aspect of this small but profitable trade in chips was that under English tax law the profit on missing chips is tax-free. The profit we made—either $1.50 or $1.30 depending on whether we gave a chain with the chip—was untaxed income. This was because the Inland Revenue agreed that the holder of the chip could bring it in and play with it, or cash it, at any time in the future. So, technically it was still a liability to the casino.

When we opened I knew very little about running a casino and less about gambling. I still don't think of myself as a gambler. I bet mostly on sure things. I'm a very skilled backgammon player and have over the years made substantial money on my game, for which I pay substantial taxes to the USA. An individual's gambling winnings are not taxable in Britain. My accountant tells me that over a three-year period, the tax on my backgammon winnings exceeded half a million dollars.

At the Playboy Club there were no doubt some likely backgammon pigeons wandering about. Alas, they were out of range, for it's against the law for an executive director to gamble in his own club. If he does, it might be to encourage other players; that is known as being a "shill." So my backgammon playing took place at my flat in London or at my country home, and in other parts of the world. At Playboy-Park Lane there was no place for backgammon, and we had no tables set aside for it. Gaming to me is simply a form of high-priced entertainment. Most people who gamble expect to lose. They can afford it. And they enjoy it. Every generation throws up new wealth, economic anomalies, those people with more money than they know what to do with. Some spend their money in casinos from sheer lack of interest in the other things money can buy.

An interesting point for sociologists is that while many of the new rich have no interest in buying great art or spending their wealth in other ways, they do see the wisdom of giving their children the best and most expensive education available. The result is that the second generation discriminate far more. They are the ones who buy the works of Picasso, Balthus, Bugatti, Wedgwood and Tiffany.

Another truth about habitual gamblers, I believe, is that many have been seduced by a lucky win early on in life. John Dante is an example.

When Playboy gave me the go-ahead to open in London with a gaming casino, in which specially trained bunny-croupiers would operate the tables, Arnie Morton sent over John Dante. Dante, a personal friend of Hefner's, had owned and operated his own club in

Chicago before he joined Playboy. It was called "Dante's Inferno."
He has always been a heavy gambler. He was one of the victims, I
discovered, of an early win.

He found the urge to risk almost every cent he earned on the turn
of a card or the speed of a horse irresistible. I knew his losses were
often fairly sizeable. "But do you ever win? I asked him.

Dante told me: "Well, once when I was very young I went to the
races with only $20 and came back with $18,000." He looked at me
sadly. "Maybe that was the worst thing that ever happened to me,
Victor. Ever since, I have been trying to repeat that win—only now I
more often go with $18,000 and come back with $20!"

I was to learn that gaming is essentially an accounting business.
Over a period of time a casino can rely on certain mathematical
percentages prevailing. With the aid of today's computers, these fine
shadings and margins can be flexibly operated to take account of
almost any tide in the money flow. The chief danger is from any
irregularity, such as can occur when an employee finds some way to
rip off the management. And in spite of minute policing by closed-
circuit television, this can still occur if casino supervision is not
efficient.

I recognized from the start that temptations abound in casinos. So
the necessity for an iron-fisted kind of rule is absolute. Men who run
casinos are paid well for their services but there are large amounts of
cash around all the time, with no inventory controls against which to
balance them. For instance, I'm sure that each of the managers at
every one of the casinos along the Strip in Las Vegas makes more
than the governor of the state. And whereas civil servants and other
state employees can be tightly controlled, catching a crooked casino
manager is a complex operation. There are occasions when one may
have to sanction a continuing fraud in order to capture culprits at
work. How can the state make a decision such as that?

While thousands of pounds or dollars are floating away there is no
time to conduct civil service hearings and appeals over whether or
not to transfer or discharge an employee. And if my constant

stressing of the possibility of these dangers in the gaming business makes it sound as if legalized casino gaming is taking a tiger by the tail, that is precisely what it is. The important thing is that having caught the tail, you know how to handle the animal to get him into the cage. What I can tell you is that getting into the cage with him is no way to run a gaming business.

So I do not believe that state ownership would ever be advisable. But I do believe that the state must provide sophisticated legal restrictions and regulations on gaming. This is not because all casino operators are thieves, or all players dishonest, but because casino gambling is what it is—the tangible expression of a very volatile aspect of human nature.

Yet until the law was changed and the 1968 Act became law in 1970, anyone could operate a game of chance without a license in England. All that we required for the Park Lane premises was a liquor licence and town planning permission for a club. And the barrister we briefed to represent our application for the latter, Victor Durand, QC, had not been told of our gaming plans. When an inveterate campaigner against all liquor licences, the Rev. Davies, opposed our licence—suggesting that having our bunny waitresses serve drinks would add to the temptations of the devil and might well lead to further horrors such as gambling—Durand jumped to his feet and declared that we had no intention of any gaming taking place in the Club. It took a further three months, and a fresh application backed by impeccable character references, to get the record straight—that we might want to introduce gaming after all. And even then we had a running fight on our hands against do-gooders like Raymond Blackburn, ex-MP and self-proclaimed ex-alcoholic, who was a source of continuing irritation.

Maybe if the 1968 Gaming Act had been in existence then— requiring gaming as well as liquor licences—we would never have aspired to include gaming in the Club. But it is interesting to note that when the new law (which, through the Casino Association, I assisted in putting together) went on the Statute Book, only 131 licences in the entire UK were granted and Playboy received one of them, because, from the start, I laid it down that our tables were to be run with scrupulous honesty and complete observance of the law.

I set up controls. No major decision involving sums of money or the cashing of checks could be taken by one of our managers or croupiers without the required number of responsible signatures approving it. Only if nearly the whole of my middle management team had been in league against us could they have got away with any scam.

When the new Act came into force, it introduced stringent regulations such as forbidding alcohol in the gaming rooms, tipping at the gaming tables, advertising, and a number of other measures. At the insistence of the Gaming Board, our cocktail-bunny costumes had to be redesigned for the bunny croupiers. The new uniform covered them up to the neck. In every way, we bent over backwards to conform to the new rules to the letter and, more importantly, to the spirit.

But the tightest laws are no proof against human mischief. In Chicago, before we ever got into gaming, our Playboy Club had attracted attention because it was patronized by some known gangsters. Columnist Sandy Smith of the *Chicago Tribune* wrote that Sam Giancana, a notorious Mafioso (later gunned down while dining in his kitchen), was an occasional user of the Club. As I told Arnie Morton: "On the one hand we are told by the law not to discriminate in our membership and on the other the press is leaping up and down and saying 'Terrible people have been seen in the Club!'" How could Hefner, whose belief in a nondiscriminatory policy was absolute, refuse to admit a man because of his notorious reputation, provided he behaved himself while in the Club?

In addition to Giancana, several of Chicago's renowned "gorillas" did use the Club from time to time. There was no way we could legally keep them out. But Smith's press attack was so damaging that we knew we had to do something about it.

We had a slotted board made and set it up at the Club entrance, reading "At the Playboy Club Tonight." Members' names were engraved on eight inch metal strips and when a member came into the Club, his name was slid into slots on the board for all to see. We figured that known crooks wouldn't want to have their presence in a club advertised at the entrance. I guessed this would keep the Mafia out. I guessed wrong.

The "At the Playboy Club" board scheme didn't work because gangster members simply gave us phony names. We couldn't ask them for birth certificates. So we were back where we started. And when Sandy Smith next came in, I asked him: "Why doesn't the government get these people off the streets—and our necks—if they are so awful? Why should a public nightclub or restaurant be expected to indict, judge and punish lawbreakers? It's the government's responsibility." He printed my comments.

A few nights later I was in another club in the Rush Street area, a nightclub where I thought I was completely unknown. A bottle of champagne was brought over to my table. "Who is this from?" I asked the waiter. "The gentleman at the bar, Mr. Giancana, sent it with his compliments," I was told. "He says he liked what you said in the paper."

It has never been Hefner's policy or mine to let criminals get within a mile of our business. And, perhaps surprisingly, very few have tried. But once, early on in Playboy's successful climb, a well-known Chicago gangster did come to see Hefner on "business." With him was an Englishman he introduced as his banker. They were interested, he said, in lending money to Playboy.

Hef heard them out politely. Then he said: "You have your enemies, and we have our enemies. If they ever got together, that would be terrible."

At that time not only was the Church waging a moral campaign against us, but our most violent opponents included the National Order for Decent Literature and many other sanctimonious organizations. Hef's shady visitors, of course, had all crime prevention and police forces solidly against them. His clear-sighted reasons for refusing any association or amalgamation made a lot of sense even to those greedy men. We heard no more from that or any other crime syndicate, nor has Playboy been bothered to this day.

Once we got into gaming, however, there were other problems. Do-gooders like Blackburn were doing their best to paint our casinos, our bunnies and every aspect of our operation in lurid colors. Fortunately, Sir Stanley Raymond, first chairman of Britain's Gaming Board, was an understanding man. I went with Sir Stanley and others of his Board when they were invited to Washington to give their views on and experiences of British gaming to the Senate Sub-committee investigating gaming in the US. I knew him to be a wise and sensible fellow. Also I gathered that our gaming operation had impressed him favorably.

So, as well as a few loud-mouthed enemies, we had powerful friends. Ironically, now that Playboy has everything I and my staff built up so carefully during the fifteen years of our British operation, we still have those friends. As Group Captain Steve Stephens, Secretary of the British Casino Association, told me the other day: "Both Field Marshal Lord Harding, the Association's chairman, and I would back your return to our industry. We're confident that you've always behaved with integrity. When Playboy threw you out, the Gaming Board lost its best friend."

At the time, my colleagues in Chicago certainly had nothing to complain about. "Average return on capital for London casinos is about 450 per cent," a leading English stockbroker, Michael Spencer of Simon and Coates, declared in 1979. "On a good casino, it can run up to 900 per cent." In our case—and we were a *very good* casino—the average often topped this glamorous figure. In the year Spencer was talking about, Playboy Clubs worldwide lost $5 million outside Britain. We turned in profits of $26 million. I had developed the Playboy casino to where it was the most profitable casino in the world.

Our financial manager in London at that time, John Wintle, told me: "We are 28 per cent ahead of last year—even without the Iranians." The Iranians were some of our biggest players. They were good (uncomplaining) losers. They vanished after the revolution.

Until 1981 we also had a surprising ally, the British Customs and Excise authorities. Instead of their winnings being taxed, as is done in other countries, Playboy paid about $44,000 a year for each table in the casino, as "gaming license duty." And that, together with UK Corporation Tax of some 50 per cent of net profits, was all the British Treasury took from us.

The rules were certainly strict, but provided we operated within them, our seat at Britain's Big Table of gaming was shaping up as a bonanza for the parent company. Only one other hurdle stood in our way at the beginning, and we found an easy way round it. The Gaming Board raised objection to the foreign control of our operation, so we formed a British Trust which, while it was responsible for running our UK interests, was in fact financially responsible to the parent company, Playboy Enterprises. The interesting point was that I was henceforward a trustee of the British Trust and, as far as management was concerned, answerable to it ahead of my parent company.

None of this concerned me at the time. The job I had created for myself as Britain's premier casino operator settled into a testing but always excitingly varied routine. As the Playboy Club and Casino expanded with the fantastic invasion of oil-rich Arabs in the seventies, I found myself running an outfit which not only produced the richest rewards and profits of the Playboy empire but more than made up for some of its huge losses.

The magnitude of the operation restricted my activities. My deputy Bill Gerhauser was directly concerned with running the gaming while my executive control placed full confidence in him and the rest of our hand-picked staff. It meant that the day-to-day running of the casinos seldom came within my orbit, though I made it a practice to take a stroll through the gaming rooms each evening I was in England.

The essence of Hefner's Playboy philosophy—freedom to enjoy pleasures earned through work and success—became a delightful reality. I was living a delightful life as the playboy extraordinary of Playboy.

Chapter Six

ROMAN SCANDALS

A few months after the London Club opened, I was at the New York Playboy Club with actress Joanna Pettet when I got a telephone call from Preuss and Morton. They told me a decision had been made not to open any more Clubs in Europe, and that after six months they wouldn't need my services.

I had been living in England for three years. In another year (in those days you needed four years to establish residency) I would have a resident's permit. My reaction to being given notice distressed me but I did need my time in Britain if I was going to be able to stay there permanently and pursue other plans.

"How would it be if I worked a full year at half pay?" I offered "That way, you'd be paying me only as much overall as it would cost you to give me six months' notice." At that time I was only getting my $50,000 a year salary, so it would cut me down to $25,000 for my last year with Playboy.

They agreed. And I had no particularly strong feelings about it either way. Provided I could work in the United Kingdom, which my resident's permit would guarantee, I had a lot of interesting possibilities ahead of me. Particularly in films.

My friendships with Roman Polanski and Gene Gutowski had led to plans for me to go into film production with them. I had a fair amount of capital stashed away from the liquidation of my 25 per cent share in Playboy Clubs. It looked as if my partnership with

Hugh Hefner was going to end and a partnership with Roman Polanski was about to begin. But it was not to be. Playboy wisely decided not to turf me out and my friendship with Polanski was to continue for five more years before ending abruptly.

Flash forward. Just after I was fired the phone rang in the living-room at Stocks. There was a call from the kitchen. They had Roman Polanski on the line from Paris.

"Do you want to talk to him?"

I had to think about it for a moment. Did I? I hadn't spoken to Roman for ten years. Now it was June 1981 and the last time that I had spoken to him was in February 1971. "Yes. Put him on the line."

"Victor, this is Roman. I'm in Paris and I've been hearing about what happened at Playboy. I want to tell you that I'm very sorry to hear what they've done to you." This was really strange, for something had come between Roman and myself. Playboy had produced and financed Roman's first movie after the tragedy in California that strangely mirrored the grotesque violence in some of his own films. The film Playboy backed was Roman's version of *Macbeth*. And even here the critics felt that the violence was a bit too specific and visible.

From the time Roman left Poland and came to live in England in 1964, I had been one of his closest friends. So what happened to terminate the friendship and why was he calling me now?

The Manson murders took place in 1969—when Roman's wife, Sharon Tate, then eight months pregnant, was murdered along with their friends, Jay Sebring, Abigail Folger and Wojtek Frykowski in the house Roman rented in Los Angeles. Roman's life had been thrown into complete confusion.

He hadn't wanted to work on any of the movies that he identified with the period before the tragedy. He lost interest in one major project, *The Day of the Dolphins,* because of his lack of con-centration, and he buried himself away, trying to forget the terrible events up in Benedict Canyon on Cielo Drive. It was, of course, impossible to put it all out of his mind, not only because of the personal impact but because the papers and magazines were full of stories, theories and replays of the tragedy. It wasn't until December of that year that the Manson gang was arrested. Once again the case occupied the headlines and made it difficult for Roman to concentrate on a new project.

Nevertheless, Roman and Bill Tennant, his agent, were searching for the right vehicle to enable him to get back to work. Roman knew Ken Tynan, the critic and writer.

He approached Ken about working on a film based on Shakespeare's *Macbeth*. Tynan became interested and agreed. It was understood between them that while they worked on *Macbeth* they would never discuss the murders in Los Angeles or politics. Ken Tynan, unlike Roman, was sympathetic to left-wing movements. Roman, who had lived under communism, was exceedingly conservative.

When they finished the scenario, I read it and was impressed. I talked to Hefner and got him to agree to back the movie, which would be the first effort of the newly formed Playboy Productions. The film was budgeted at $1,500,000 and we got a completion guarantee on it. This meant that if Roman went over budget or appeared to be going over budget he would be removed and another director would be brought in to complete it and he would lose his equity in the film's profits, if any.

Roman had every reason to want to finish the film within budget. True to form, he ran way over and Playboy was faced with an agonizing decision. Either we could invoke the completion guarantee which meant he would be replaced as director or we could stick with Roman and invest additional funds.

Polanski, as far as I was concerned, was acting like a small child. This was embarrassing for me personally since I had persuaded Hefner to back him. My personal dilemma was resolved by Hefner, who agreed to pay the overages and allow Roman to finish the film in his own time. He even agreed to let Roman keep his equity in the finished work.

Unfortunately, Roman did not choose to repay Hefner's magnanimity with anything resembling gratitude. Just before the film opened, Roman spoke to Stanley Edwards of the *Evening Standard*.

The interview was held in Playboy Club's VIP Room and Polanski was quoted as saying: "I really don't like it here."

Edwards commented that he felt that this was a rather unkind thing to say in view of the fact that Playboy's chairman, Hugh Hefner, had put up the money for Roman's film.

Roman replied by saying *"pecunia non olet"* which means "money doesn't smell"—a way you would refer to money that came from a tainted source.

I hit the roof. Not only was this not the way to talk about a friend, but it was lousy business as far as the film itself was concerned. We deserved better, and Roman's reference to our money smelling was totally undeserved.

After that, there was only one more thing I had to do with Roman and that was to introduce him, along with the stars of the movie, to Princess Anne at the Royal Première on 2 February 1971 at the Plaza Theatre in London. After I had presented just about everybody who had played a major role in putting the film together I came to Roman, who couldn't resist telling Princess Anne, "I'll never again make a film that has horses in it." Polanski insisted that horses simply could not be directed the way actors could.

Even though I couldn't help laughing at Roman's joke, I felt terrible about the way the situation had disintegrated. Not only would the film not recover its original investment for Playboy, but Polanski was unwilling to help us promote the film. As I wrote to Hefner at the time, "The thing that's so distressing to me is that for years I did everything I possibly could to be helpful to the son of a bitch and only recently have I come to realize that I was merely being exploited by him."

One of the clues had been the fact that in the interview that he gave to *Playboy* magazine, he didn't mention me except to suggest to the interviewer that they go to a party that I was having at my house and see if he and the interviewer could pick up some girls.

I told Hefner how much I appreciated the fact that he hadn't taken me to task for my bad judgment in selling this project to Playboy, and I said in closing, "The fact that you don't proves to me, as always, that you are my very best friend."

I broke off my friendship with Roman and I sent back to him the few gifts I'd received from him over the years, including a solid gold prick that he and Sharon had given me as a thank-you present for hosting their wedding reception. Polanski had this crafted in Los Angeles and he had actually smuggled it through Customs in his trousers with the thought in mind that if he was caught he would claim that it was a necessary artificial limb. I sent it back to him with a note which said: "In view of recent developments I no longer care to have this full-length, lifesize portrait of you around the house. I'm sure you will have no difficulty finding some 'friend' you can shove it up."

Now ten years later here was Polanski on the telephone and a situation that was completely reversed. Hefner, who I had said at the time was my very best friend, had completely betrayed me and Roman was calling to extend his hand in friendship. What a switch!

Over the years that I knew him my friendship with Roman had been deep and continuous. We met at Cannes through a mutual friend, his producer, Gene Gutowski, and the friendship began. I could not speak any of the languages Roman already knew well— Polish, Russian, French, Italian and even German (which he generally pretended not to understand at all). In fact, I only speak English, so my relationship with Roman was somewhat limited at first as he was just learning English. He would try out his newly acquired vocabulary by telling jokes and watching the reaction of his audience to see if they were forcing laughter or if they genuinely understood the humor. If the message got across and the laughter was sincere, Roman took it as a sure sign that his mastery of English was improving. Roman appreciated criticism and as I was a student of joke-telling (at one time I edited *Playboy's Party Jokes*) I would patiently explain to him where the joke went wrong in translation.

The two of us used to hang around a lot together when we weren't working. We both were bachelors and we enjoyed the same sort of thing—the discothèques, skiing in the Alps in winter time and lolling around in the South of France during the summer. Roman met Sharon at a party at my house in Montpelier Square. She was a house guest who had been referred to me by her then-boyfriend, Jay Sebring.

The night before he found out about Sharon's and Jay's murder in Los Angeles, Roman and I had been together with writer-photographer Peter Beard (who married and is now divorced from model Cheryl Tiegs).

We had all been at a discothèque called the Revolution in Bruton Place, with no thought that Roman's wife and our friends in California were only a few hours away from death. After we'd heard of the murders, I accompanied Roman to Los Angeles to bury Sharon.

Thinking back on it all, I tried to analyze what makes Roman the way he is. First of all, there is the fact that he initially found acceptance as a sort of precocious child. And because of his small stature—friends used to tell us that we looked like father and son together—Roman has held on to that image of the precocious child throughout adulthood.

Even today his Polish friends call him Romek, that's the diminutive for Roman, and in a funny kind of way I think that even though he is attractive to girls who are a head and shoulders taller than him, he feels more on an even footing with petite girls or very young girls.

That helps to explain Roman's involvement with under-age girls like the one whose seduction brought him to court in Los Angeles and ultimately made him a fugitive from justice living in France. But how does it explain his generally "rip-off" kind of attitude towards society in general and even towards his closest friends?

Well, I think you have to make allowances for all the tragedy in Roman's life. His mother died in Auschwitz. One story has it that Roman himself survived because his mother threw him off the truck that was taking the two of them to the concentration camp. He was eight at the time.

Shortly after the war ended and after Roman was reunited with his father, his father cast him out of their home because a new stepmother didn't want him around. A while later, he had his skull fractured when he was beaten, robbed and almost killed by someone who led him into an underground location where he was supposedly going to show Roman a bicycle that he wanted to sell.

Ever the saucy little lad, Roman progressed to a brilliant career as an actor and then as a highly successful director. But tragedy seemed still to stalk him, culminating in the awful Manson murders in 1969. It is small wonder that a man so abused should develop such an intensely self-centered personality. When I fell out with him, my then close friend Hefner spoke very compassionately of Polanski. But Hefner, a student in psychology, regarded him as self-destructive and insecure, incapable of sustaining a close relationship for any length of time. I guess one can only pray that the world will ultimately treat Roman in a fair and understanding way and that little Romek will eventually become a fully fledged adult Roman. I, for one, sincerely hope so.

Roman did introduce me to Connie Kreski, a beautiful, fragile-looking blonde who became *Playboy*'s Playmate of the Year in 1969. She'd been a model and, in a small way, a film actress. She'd also trained as a nurse but, after graduating, dropped that career because she couldn't stand the sight of blood.

I'd met up with her when both Roman and I were guests at Hefner's Chicago mansion. I invited her to come to England and stay with me. Soon after she arrived she met Anthony Newley, who was making a strangely titled film, *Can Hieronymus Merkin Ever Forget Mercy Humppe and Find True Happiness?* He saw her in the elevator going up to my office and offered her the title part which suited her ideally.

Emphasizing the ethereal quality Connie has—like a blonde, blue-eyed fairy floating about in a dreamy landscape—she was only seen in the film in misty scenes, underwater in the nude or in a pink party dress on a carousel. I delighted in her but Connie could never adjust to my penchant for the company of more than one girl at a time.

I'd moved to No. 1 Connaught Square in 1967, having lost

Montpelier Square when a friend, John Pringle, bought the house after I passed it up. In the new place there were three guest bedrooms and a master bedroom and I often had the house filled with glamorous guests. I'm afraid Connie just couldn't stand the stress.

I liked to have all the friends who came to stay with me joining in the fun at mealtimes, watching the 16 mm movies I projected after dinner and just socializing. But Connie wasn't the type. She liked us to be alone. One lovely little friend of mine, Jan Ross, who was a bunny until she became a Clermont receptionist, had to quit when Connie got upset about some real or imagined escapade. I was so fond of Connie that I would have done a great deal to please her.

But pleasing her wasn't possible. She took Valium to relieve her tension and it seemed to make her worse. She went back to the States, though I still regarded her as my special girl. In fact, when I went through Los Angeles on my way to my daughter's wedding in Tacoma, Washington, in the summer of 1973, Connie joined me. But that was the last act for us.

She'd taken up with the film actor, James Caan, and they became a Hollywood "item." On the trip she told me that all was over between us. Later Jimmy suddenly married another girl. Connie just has very bad luck with men. I saw her a year ago and she was as beautiful as ever.

Chapter Seven
PARADISE FOUND

My romance wth Connie had come during the time of my crucial career decision, while Hef's Chicago management team were counting the dollars and cents from our operation in London and preparing to let me go. I couldn't blame them. Even though the London Club was already showing a healthy profit (on an investment of only one and a half million dollars, we were to achieve pre-tax profits of close on a million in that first year), the overall health of the company was making them sensitive to any fresh and speculative investment. If there wasn't going to be any expansion ... they didn't need me.

If I hadn't wanted to establish my British position, I might well have accepted the logic of the situation. Fortunately I had bought time at the cost of half my annual salary. During that period, the success I had always believed would be due to the Club became undeniable. Before my time had run out, I was, even in their view, invaluable—heading Playboy's most profitable operation.

And Hef stepped in at once. He personally made Preuss, Morton and the others tear up the agreement I'd signed to take my leave. The threat was cancelled. Ironically, I can now look back on the fact that Arnie Morton and Bob Preuss got the heave-ho before me.

Morton was forced out because he was always at odds with Bob Preuss over management policy. After he left he founded the Chicago area's most successful group of up-market restaurants—

Arnie's, Morton's and Zorine's. He's become a highly visible civic leader, a great friend of Mayor Jane Byrne, and my candidate for a national success story since he recently opened a Morton's in Washington, D.C.

Bob Preuss, on the other hand, didn't leave until one year after Morton. He departed in 1975, when the company seemed to be in serious financial trouble. Hef, who had sided with Preuss against Morton, was troubled by Bob's failure. Personally I always thought Bob tried to do too much. He didn't like to delegate, couldn't delegate and when problems arose he was crushed.

When, a few years after they were both gone, Hef explained to me how he viewed the sequence of events, he gave me some insight into how he must now perceive my own fate and the loss of Playboy's English interests. Hef didn't admit that he made a mistake forcing Arnie Morton out and siding with Bob Preuss. Instead he said: "I thought Preuss was right and Morton was wrong. I didn't realize they were both wrong." Well, hell, I suppose it's pretty close to admitting a mistake.

The way things took off in London was really incredible. Thinking back, I can see that my whole life has taken a series of jumps forward as a result of crises over the years. Maybe that's an omen. I hope so. Historically, Playboy's London development was among the fastest growing and most lucrative of any seen in Britain since World War II.

In 1963, I had landed at Manchester with barely more than a suitcase. Two and a half years later the Playboy Club, which was to become one of London's landmarks, opened at 45 Park Lane. In 1970, I added the fashionable Clermont and, ten years later, the popular Victoria Sporting Club. We also went into the bookmaking business. First we established a successful credit bookmaking operation and then opened more than eighty betting shops with the familiar bunnyhead trademark. Then there were our provincial Clubs in Portsmouth and Manchester.

So, in only seventeen years, with the help of a wonderful staff, I had built Playboy's most successful operation. In 1979, an astute

Fleet Street financial editor, the late Patrick Hutber of the *Sunday Telegraph*, saw from statistics published in the United States that I was also receiving the rewards of success. Word must have got around, because someone called me up to tell me: "Look in the 1979 edition of the *Guinness Book of Records*. On page 234, you're listed as Britain's highest-paid executive."

With a certain mixture of feelings at such materialistic publicity, I did look. *Guinness* has placed me on the same page as a Frenchman, Monsieur "Mangetout," who ate a bicycle in fifteen days—an achievement certainly more bizarre than mine, though potentially just as conducive to chronic indigestion. The fact that I had become the highest-paid UK executive was more a tribute to my employers' lack of concern for intelligent tax planning (or a subtle comment on the mistrust of incentives brought about by Britain's welfare state) than anything else.

In 1972, I bought one of the finest, most satisfying possessions of my life, Stocks House. It had stood outside the Hertfordshire village of Aldbury for as long as records can be found to testify to its existence. The first mention of it was in the Domesday Book. The present building dates back to 1773 when it was erected by the Duncombe family. The nineteenth-century statesman and prime minister, Earl Grey of Falloden, inherited the property from an aunt, only to decide that as it lacked water, hence fishing, it wasn't for him.

Water had always been a problem at Stocks. In 1739 one of the Duncombes wrote a poem about the previous house on the site, ruing the absence of "bubbling brook or meandering stream." Following the descriptive verse in iambic pentameter, the resident poet added in parenthesis: "But where is the place, and who the man, that to perfection can lay just pretense?" Well, at least I installed a swimming pool.

Grey never lived at Stocks. He sold the property in 1896 to Humphry Ward, art editor of *The Times*, and his famous novelist wife, Mary Ward. Two years after I moved in, Lesley Parrish, an Englishwoman working at the US Embassy in London, asked if she could come out to see the house. She was interested in Mrs. Humphry Ward, whose books had sold millions of copies in their day (though now they are out of print). I replied on notepaper of my townhouse, No. 1 Connaught Square, and was surprised to be asked by Lesley Parrish if I had bought both properties from the Ward estate at the same time.

When I told her that there was no connection between the two, she informed me that by strange coincidence my Connaught Square house was where Mrs. Humphry Ward had died in 1920. Stocks House had then been sold first to a family named Blezard and then to a family named Brown. The Browns had kept it until Brondesbury (a private school for young ladies which took its name from the North London district where it started) bought it from them. More accurately, the head mistress Miss K. Forbes-Dunlop had acquired it in 1945. In all, the four head mistresses who had run the school during more than a century had each in turn become the proprietor of the school itself.

I bought Stocks from Miss Forbes-Dunlop, known to her students as "Bungie," and it was she who impressed me with the strong feeling of warmth and dedication that the school felt for the old place. I first went on a fine April day. For six months I had been fruitlessly searching for a suitable country house where I could stable horses. Perhaps I was unconsciously following in Hefner's footsteps, having always admired his fine mansion homes.

Actually, I'd seen an advertisement for Stocks in *Country Life*. With Karen Lamm, a petite blonde lady friend of mine who was staying in London with me, I drove in search of it. But George, my chauffeur, lost the way and by the time we arrived the students and their teachers were about to sit down to dinner. I made another trip the following day, and this time I sent my other driver, Brian, in to see if it would be convenient for us to look it over.

Brian came back looking very discouraging. "You won't like it, Mr. Lownes," he said. "The place smells of cabbage and pencilboxes."

Knowing that all schools smell like that, I wasn't put off. And when I met and talked to Miss Forbes-Dunlop and her deputy, Miss

Above The Victor Aubrey Lownes dynasty, I, II and III, photographed in 1936. I was eight at the time. *Below* Twenty-seven years later. My grandfather, who lived to be 92, joins in my eve-of-departure celebration at the New York Playboy Club in December 1963; I was shortly to sail for England.

With Mary Ann La Joie. She was the model in the background of the *Playboy* ad, "What Sort of Man Reads *Playboy*?"

Above With Shel Silverstein during my sabbatical from Playboy. Silverstein—bestselling author, songwriter, cartoonist—was a contributor to *Playboy* magazine almost from the start. His cartoon (*below*) underlines the importance of a frisky image to Playboy.

"I don't care if you call me Mr. Lownes when we're alone, but when there are other people around, you're supposed to call me baby!"

Silverstein's
**HISTORY OF
PLAYBOY**

The first six hand-picked English bunnies, photographed at my house in Montpelier Square, London. Dolly Read (on the right) was greatly attracted to entertainers; she later married Dick Martin, of *Laugh-In* fame. *Below* With actress Joanna Pettet at one of our clubs.

Above With Hugh Hefner (*left*) at a Writers' Convocation, cracking up during Art Buchwald's opening speech, October 1971; and (*below*) with Roman Polanski (*left*) and the producer Gene Gutowski (*center*) in the VIP room at London's Playboy Club. This was *before* Polanski made his offensive reference to Playboy.

Above Trainee bunny croupiers in the converted chapel at Stocks. *Below* Liberal MP Clement Freud, a non-executive director of Playboy, who was later asked to resign for a technical breach of company rules. Boxing promoter Harry Levene is on the left.

Above Peter Sellers and comedian Bill Cosby with ex-bunnies at the Playboy Club's disco, 1975.
Below Bunnies relaxing at the training school at Stocks, and being coached by Alan Kinghorn for
work in the betting shops. In the six years he ran Playboy's bookmaking division, turnover rose
from nought to £40 million.

Above left The Collinson twins, Madeline and Mary, who became the first and only Playmate double; for a time I was one of their shared interests. *Above right* When my chauffeur, Danny Gillen, married in 1978, I took the wheel. *Below* Playboy executives toast the acquisition of the Clermont Club: from left, Bernie Mulhearn, Bill Gerhauser, Victor Lownes, Peter Ryan, Wolf Gelderblom.

Thea Rose, and saw the old house and grounds, I began to be enraptured. The possibilities were there. It never occurred to me that I could really occupy such a large place, but everything I looked at made it more attractive in my eyes. In particular, I caught the contagious affection which the ladies so obviously felt for Stocks.

So I decided to buy it. I made a bid of $200,000 which was accepted, but later heard that somebody else was trying to "gazump" me. When I discovered that Miss Forbes-Dunlop and Miss Thea Rose were far too nice to listen to the new offer, having accepted mine, I upped my offer to $230,000 (a compromise figure between my original offer and the "gazumping" bid) and they were delighted.

Since then, I have done everything possible to keep together the bits and pieces reminiscent of the school days. Although I have spent something like a million dollars in various forms of improvement and restoration—rewiring, central heating, installing the jacuzzi, resurfacing the tennis court and putting in a machine for throwing practice tennis balls (as well as converting some of the rooms into games rooms for my growing collection of electronic and pinball machines)—I am far too fond of the old place and its venerable history to do anything which I think its previous owners would regard a sacrilege.

One example: before I moved in, I saw a sign in one of the school-rooms which read: "There is no Tiddle Taddle or Pibble Pabble in Pompey's Camp." I had no idea what "pibble pabble" meant, and it doesn't show up in any dictionary I have seen, but I liked the sign. I also liked what I believe it stands for. So I told the dear ladies of Brondesbury that I would like to keep it. Then, to what must have been their embarrassment, it disappeared mysteriously following their last Speech Day at the house. The next thing I knew was that an advertisement appeared in the *Daily Telegraph* asking "The person who removed the sign" to get in touch with the headmistress at once.

I thought, "Goodness—that's probably the sign I wanted!" And sure enough, one of the girls had taken it as a souvenir, thinking nobody would want it. Her name was Sophie Waddilove, and not only did she promptly return the sign, but recently she has written asking if a party could be held for Miss Forbes-Dunlop's ninetieth birthday at Stocks. I delighted in telling her that by all means there should be a party—but on no account should there be any mention of the dear headmistress's precise age. Not the sort of thing well-educated ladies should discuss. On this point I was overruled.

If Stocks had possessed only these charming details of previous life and the love of those who shared it, I might have passed it as I did the previous fifty or so English country houses I had looked at. But it possessed the accommodations I vaguely saw as appropriate to my needs. Stocks had twenty-one bedrooms, four cottages and a number of outbuildings. I had always entertained on a fairly lavish scale and enjoyed almost perpetual house parties. Its comfort and attraction made it an enviable place to stay, and I had my horses well stabled and cared for by my own staff.

One of these, master chef Antonio Masut, has been with me since 1964. Unfortunately he lost his brother-in-law in an earthquake and since then has had to support his family in Italy. This has meant that Antonio comes and goes from Stocks, his times with me depending on the harvest, the spring sowing and other chores of farm life. We have become such good friends over the years that he insists on working for me for nothing, which I regard as a great compliment.

Some time after Antonio joined me, Michael Holiday, an excellent chef, came to Stocks. He and Antonio have made the modernized kitchens their domain and Michael, who is with me all the year round, more or less runs the entire establishment, with its staff of sixteen.

So I woke up one morning in 1972 in the house where Mrs. Humphry Ward had died, and quite by accident I had come to live in her home in the country. Only later did I learn that in her last letter, written from Connaught Square, she said: "Now it is spring, and I long to return to Stocks." It was spring when I first saw her lovely home. And I have returned to it with delight ever since.

Mrs. Humphry Ward is buried nearby, in Aldenbury cemetery, and her only living grandchild—the wife of the Bishop of Ripon, Mrs. Moorman—once commented that her grandmother would "spin in her grave" if she knew who owned Stocks now. Meaning, I suppose, that Britain's renowned playboy would have shocked the great writer. Let me reassure her: Mary Ward was as much a revolutionary heretic in her day as *Playboy* is today. If she could pay me a visit, I believe we'd get along fine.

My original feeling that the place might be too spacious for me soon vanished. Two years after moving in I was adding an entire new wing. But by then I'd realized that the Company's need for premises in which to train our growing staff exceeded anything we had available in London. With some adjustments, mainly cosmetic, Stocks offered an ideal training center.

Sharing my time between this paradise and London—where I eventually moved from Connaught Square to the penthouse on top of the Club—I found it possible to expand in two directions at once. While at my London desk I was Playboy Supremo. I ruled over a kingdom of 200-300 beautiful bunnies and my highly paid expert staff. But once my chauffeur-driven Rolls turned off the M1 into the Hertfordshire countryside, I was away in a dreamland beauty.

I know a popular fantasy exists about Stocks, but it is all rubbish. In people's minds my bachelorhood, my association with Playboy, the fact that the house is full of such fun devices as an indoor jacuzzi, sauna, solarium and outdoor pool suggests that Stocks is a center for bizarre behavior. It isn't. And what amuses me is that I don't live up to people's idea of a screaming sex maniac.

The people who act in the most extreme way at Stocks—swimming nude in the pool and jacuzzi, for example—are not unlike the wife of one publishing executive who came with her husband to stay for a weekend. When he first told her that they were to be my guests, she tried to dissuade him. She said she thought that it would be a very dangerous place to visit. They would, she said, "see things such as they were unaccustomed to seeing." And their reputations, she felt, might be harmed.

As I remember it, I was forewarned that I would have to be very careful not to do anything that might offend the chap's wife. This really wasn't necessary as there is nothing at Stocks which could offend anyone during a conventional weekend. Nothing, that is, that I know about—which is not to say that I always know what people are doing in their own bedrooms. Nor do I want to know.

But it was quite funny on this occasion because, as I walked through the jacuzzi area on my way from the conservatory into the discothèque late in the evening, I noticed that one topless—and bottomless—swimmer was frolicking in the pool. Surprisingly, it was the lady who was concerned about what Stocks might do to her reputation.

In point of fact I have no objection to someone enjoying the jacuzzi nude late in the evening, if they like to do so. But I might object if they chose to do it in the daytime when there are almost always young children around. House parties at Stocks, as at every other ordinary English country house of any size, are family affairs.

I have of course been privileged to entertain a whole host of celebrated and fascinating guests, but these are not always the most entertaining or amusing. I certainly don't invite them to spend a weekend with me because of their famous names, even though my visitors' book at Stocks would make any autograph-hunter's mouth water, I'm sure.

While I was in America working for *Playboy* I met and got to know a great many movie stars and showbusiness personalities. In 1970 I produced the first Monty Python film in England which put me in touch with the film business in Britain as well as the wonderful Monty Python gang. At that time the American producer of *A Touch of Class* and other great movies, Mel Frank, was living down the street from me and he introduced me to Lee Marvin, George Segal and others. My place became something of a center for visiting American movie stars while they were working in Britain, and my own growing interest as a producer brought me in contact with many British artists. Through Roman Polanski I met the late Peter Sellers who became a great friend and one I shall always miss.

I remember that Peter was in Cortina one Christmas; whereas he himself was not too keen on the skiing, he was good company—especially when he played Santa Claus for all of us at the chalet. Unlike most of the comedians I have known over the years, he enjoyed being very funny in private. Most comedians, like Woody Allen, Lenny Bruce and Mort Sahl, are virtually tragic figures when they're off stage, but Peter was always entertaining.

The real Sellers was difficult to perceive. He was constantly taking on the characters of the people he portrayed in his role as actor. But I did occasionally get a glimpse of what the real Peter Sellers was like. When he stayed at Stocks one weekend, he strenuously complained of the quality of my sound system, and he felt that a better amplifier would mightily improve the records and tapes we were playing. I nodded in agreement.

At six o'clock the following morning he leaped out of bed, raced into town, took an amplifier out of his own hi-fi rig and raced back to Stocks. When we got up around ten we already had an improved quality of sound. I was surprised that a star of Sellers' magnitude would do something like that, but at the same time, and more revealing of his personality perhaps, was that he didn't offer to give or sell the amplifier to me. As soon as the weekend was over he packed it up and took it away with him.

Peter came to several of my New Year's Eve parties, and the hunt crowd were very impressed to see him. He took a strong liking to Mai Britt (who used to work at the Clermont Club), and one of the few photographs I managed to take of him over the years shows him photographing Mai on the back porch at Stocks.

After the problem I had with Roman and the embarrassment his *Macbeth* movie led to with Hefner, I never again suggested that

Playboy invest in film projects in which I was personally interested. But for myself, I'm always interested in a play or movie I think is worthwhile, especially if it is likely to make money. Not all of them have. I've backed a few losers in my time, but always with at least some personal satisfaction.

The Monty Python series was a success in all ways. As an American I felt that it would go over in the States, but I was a little wary of having been in England too long—seven years—to be still totally American in my tastes and point of view. When I talked to the show's animator, Terry Gilliam, about it and discussed the comedy routines with John Cleese, Graham Chapman and others, I told them: "Some of the gags go on too long for American audiences. You'd better let me trim them."

As I was putting up the whole of the money for the picture (less than $400,000 actually) and was executive producer, I had a free hand. Whatever Python material of the period is missing from that first Monty Python movie—entitled *And Now for Something Completely Different*—is due to my editing. I had to cut out some good stuff, notably the "flying sheep" sequence, but I believe the movie was improved by the cutting. It has made money for me ever since and I could almost live on what it makes even today. I gave a piece of it to my son Val. Another piece helped an American ex-Playmate, Gloria Root, to complete her architectural studies. Gloria came to England, where I met her, after an unpleasant experience. She had been in a Greek jail for a year convicted of drug charges. I thought she needed help more than most.

Today the film has a life of its own. In the States it has become a cult film and I expect to see it on video any day now. If anybody wants to criticize the cuts I made they should first talk to my friend Woody Allen. I got to know him when I was living in Montpelier Square, while he was making *Casino Royale* in London. We kept in touch and he came over on another visit while I was making my Monty Python movie which interested him both because it was a comedy and because he, too, was an admirer of the Python series.

Woody asked me one day how long the finished film was in its rough-cut state and I told him: "One hundred and seven minutes."

Woody said: "Go clip." His belief, he told me, is that "no comedy
movie should run for more or less than eighty-eight minutes. That is
the precise length an audience wants." So I took his advice and
trimmed even more.

A lady named Pat Casey produced the movie. But when we were
getting down to titles, Terry Gilliam refused to give me "executive
producer" credit. So, in deference to my achievement, I went
outside and had one made which must be the most monumental
solo-frame credit of all time—a blockbusting, three-dimensional
title, a copy of which hangs on my wall in Stocks to commemorate
my little bit of movie history.

The Monty Python gang got back at me for this by using my name
as "producer in charge of titles" on one of their own shows as a gag
on television. And then, in their album *The Contractual Obligation
Album,* they did a little skit which is obviously dedicated to me
because it is entitled *The Gospel According to St. Victor;* and at the
end of it I am leading one of the comely angels off to a jacuzzi.

Ken Tynan had asked me to put money into the original London
production of *Oh, Calcutta,* but Hilly Elkins had rushed it onto the
stage in New York so that by the time I got around to investing in it
in London it was already a Broadway hit. Ken's idea was that
Playboy should back the show, but I'd told him he would have to
approach Hefner himself on anything like that. Later on, I did take a
piece of the London production on my own behalf. I gathered, by
the way, that Ken's title had been taken from the French *'O, quel cul
tu as!'*—literally, 'Oh, what an ass you have!'

Thanks to Ken Tynan, I lost money on the Rolf Hochhuth play
Soldiers, but this didn't bother me. Like Ken, I thought this story of
how Churchill could have saved the life of the free-Polish World War
II hero, General Sikorski, and didn't, should be brought to the
stage. Though it flopped, I still believed it deserved an audience.

After I bought Stocks and was able to invite so many more people
to spend weekends with me, the house filled a valuable role both as
a meeting-place for discussing some of these ventures and as a place
of fun and relaxation. Look inside the visitors' book and you'll see
Miss Piggy and Kermit the Frog—even Animal—which probably

has something to do with the fact that both Jim Henson and Frank Oz have been frequent visitors. With Michael White, the very clever young British producer who brought *Chorus Line* to London—and who, incidentally, grabbed the Monty Python idea after my lead for his successful *Monty Python and the Holy Grail* movie—I talked about *Annie* when he was bringing that over as well. I bought into that show which I am happy to say is still paying dividends. I should thank Stocks for that one too.

So, some people's impression of my life as a Rabelaisian romp with no serious purpose is a parody of the truth. If I have enjoyed the company of more famous people than most, entertaining and keeping open house for some of the world's superstars—Warren Beatty, Jack Nicholson, Peter Cook and Valerie Perrine have been fairly regular visitors over the years—this has not altered the fact that Stocks, for me, was always a delightful home where my friends and I could enjoy all that it has to offer.

Tony Curtis is an occasional visitor, and he can be very amusing and funny. He likes to get all the guests together and improvise a highly dramatic play with himself as director and everybody making up their own dialogue.

Tony likes wearing a white cowboy hat, and when he stays at Stocks we frequently go riding in the Chiltern Hills and down to the village of Aldbury. My horse is a few yards behind Tony's, and I'm always trailing behind him. People point to him in the street and say "Is that . . .? is that . . .?" trying to figure out who he is, and I come along and say "Tony Curtis" out of the side of my mouth.

It is funny how most people have difficulty recognizing celebrities out of context. The Hertfordshire villagers point at Tony Curtis and stammer "Why that's . . .? that's . . .?" until I fill in the blank. Once we provided a similarly humbling experience for Gene Hackman at The Greyhound pub in Aldbury. A local came over to our table and said to Gene: "You can settle a little bet I have with my friends; you're the movie star, aren't you?" Gene nodded humbly; then the fan shouted triumphantly to his friends at the back, "See, I told you it was Rod Steiger!"

I was on a British Airways plane to Malaga with Barbara Parkins a few years ago when the steward stopped at our seats and started telling Barbara what a fan his wife was, and how much she'd treasure her autograph, because she never missed an episode of *Peyton Place* on TV. Barbara graciously penned a personalized note to the steward's wife and then signed her name at the bottom. The steward looked crushed, hesitated and then said: "Could you do it over, and just sign it 'Betty Anderson'? She won't know who Barbara Parkins is." I'm sure Larry Hagman must constantly be asked: "Forget the Hagman tag—just sign it J.R."

I met Peter Cook many years ago when he first came to America and attempts were being made to sell *Private Eye* to Playboy. In those days it wasn't the success that it is now. Peter knew of us through our association with Lenny Bruce, who had played in the club Peter also owned in Soho called The Establishment.

About a year later I rushed into a theatre in New York to see Peter in *Beyond the Fringe*. I had caught a plane in Los Angeles, raced to New York, leapt into a taxi cab and zoomed to the theatre, where I had tickets booked—only I walked into the wrong show. I was sitting in my seat watching a play that had nothing to do with *Beyond the Fringe,* and after about five minutes of wondering what the hell was going on I looked at the program in my lap and found I was at the wrong play. So I rushed out and asked the lady in the lobby where *Beyond the Fringe* was playing, and she explained it was next door.

Everywhere I have lived since starting the London Club has been happily crowded with beautiful girls and entertaining people, no doubt the one helping to attract the other. Montpelier Square, Connaught Square, Stocks and the Playboy penthouse have never lacked pleasant company.

Some of my friends have known all these homes of mine. Marilyn Cole, a long-time friend, who has been a regular visitor for the past ten years, was a bunny in the early seventies who first caught my eye when I was taking her photograph. Not a thing I usually did, but on this occasion I had a new camera that I wanted to try out. So I asked the bunny mother to let me take the routine pictures required for employment records of the latest girls. And by good fortune Marilyn was among them.

Marilyn stood out from the rest, partly because she was un-selfconscious. She had wonderfully long, slim legs and an extremely beautiful figure.

One of the reasons why Playboy Clubs have always had a high turnover in bunnies is that many of the girls have been spoiled. Because they are so pretty and have such wonderful figures they are shocked when they find they actually have to work.

"You mean I have to carry this tray? You mean I really have to deal these cards as well as be beautiful? My goodness, this isn't for me!"

It's a sad fact about beauty, which we tend to ignore. But I gather scientists are now making a study of the effects of beauty on a person's career, so perhaps we—and they—will learn more about this phenomenon.

Marilyn's unique quality is that she *is* beautiful—outstandingly so—but she has always, since leaving school, worked hard for her living without any suggestion that she should not have to do so. Before she became a bunny, she had a job in the Portsmouth Co-op. She has a mind very much of her own. And although we have enjoyed a lot of fun together and a lot of high living in various parts of the world, she has always kept her feet on the ground, her independence, and—significantly—her own apartment.

As a matter of fact, it was the photograph I took that started Marilyn on an eventful career. I thought she looked so great that I asked a German professional photographer, Frank Habicht, who had brought some possible Playmate pictures into the office to take a series of pictures of Marilyn to send to Hefner. He was knocked out by them. Would I send Marilyn over to Chicago immediately? "Fine," I told him, "but should I accompany her, perhaps?"

The message came back: "No need." Obviously, Hef shared my interest in getting to know Marilyn better. Maybe he thought this might be kind of uphill if her discoverer were hanging around.

Anyway, I dispatched Marilyn to Chicago with no hard feelings. And while she was in Chicago I heard that her friendship with Hef had developed romantically.

In the months that she was off and on in Chicago, not only did she become one of our most popular Playmates, but she and Hef were seen together a great deal. As I told her later this rather amused me, because I knew that Hefner had two serious lady friends at the time, Karen Christy in Chicago and Barbie Benton in Los Angeles.

"So what?" Marilyn said. "How do you think my boyfriend feels when he sees the pictures of me with Hefner?" Back in Portsmouth apparently Marilyn had a serious suitor.

I think I realized then how much I liked Marilyn's ways.

Playmates were very special people in the company. When they were picked, always by Hefner personally, it was not unlike being selected for a starring role in a movie. Marilyn was one of only three British girls who have ever made it to date—and the only one to be "Playmate of the Year." Most of the girls who appeared in the centerfold of *Playboy* magazine over the years were discovered by photographers, agencies and studios. Rewards were considerable.

Once she had passed through an intensive selection process, a Playmate was invited to sign a contract with the company. In return for what was then a fee of $5,000, half of it to be paid on her signing the contract and the other half when her pictures appeared in the magazine, she would also be offered the opportunity to take part in a number of promotional and publicity engagements for which she would earn further fees.

Marilyn's affair with Hefner must have left him with memories of her charms. Months after Hefner had last seen her, I took her with me to the opening of the Playboy Hotel in Great Gorge, New Jersey. It was fifty miles outside New York City and was a beautiful place with four indoor tennis courts, eighteen outdoor courts and pools both inside and outside the building. In winter there were ski runs. Marilyn and I arrived looking forward to an enjoyable stay.

It was therefore quite a surprise when Dick Rosenzweig, Hefner's Number Two at the time, called me with an urgent message. There was to be a splendid opening party that night in the hotel to which I had been invited and to which, naturally, I intended taking Marilyn. Dick's message was loud and clear: "If you show up with her, Hef will be very upset." (Incidentally, Hef has recently, and wisely, reappointed Dick to the VP-at-his-elbow role. One hopes that, as in Dick's previous reign, the real world will now find its way into Hef's field of vision.)

At first I thought Dick must be joking. Hef is never short of girlfriends and he had Barbie Benton in tow for the opening; but apparently Marilyn had made such an impression on him that he couldn't bear to see her with another guy—not even with me. This, in spite of the fact that in the past we both dated the same girls without either of us being upset. I always, of course, avoided his special "number one" girls.

"Wait a minute," I told Dick. "Hef has Barbie and he knows that Marilyn has a steady boyfriend in England. Does he seriously mean that he never wants us to be seen together? This is going to prove a little difficult."

"Well," Dick said, "I can only tell you what I was ordered to tell you. Let me spell it out. Hef would be gratified if you would both stay in your room while the party is going on."

We did. And made a big joke of it. Hugh Hefner, my old buddy, was so jealous of a lady's affection that it would have spoiled his evening to see her with me! But after a day and a night hiding away in our room, the joke wore a little thin. I told Marilyn to pack. We checked out of Great Gorge and flew to the Playboy Hotel in Miami Beach, Florida. I knew we would find some fresh air down there— and I needed fresh air.

I guess Hef realized that he'd gone too far. A day or so later, he called me and we had a man-to-man chat. He'd got over the whole thing and laughed about it. "If you two are enjoying each other's company, you have my blessing," he told me. And that was the end of it. I went back to work and Marilyn and I have stayed friends ever since.

For a single man, the question of marriage is constantly alive and kicking. Many an intimate lady friend, over the years, has asked me the simple question: "Why don't we get married?" When I hear those words and see that look in the lady's eye, I have a ready answer which fends off the issue with a jest. "Great idea," I say, "but who would have us?"

Actually, I get along with women beautifully, but I'm not monogamous and I'm a bad liar. So, much as I'd like to—and there have been several girls I've been involved with for a long time who'd make super wives—I can't take the vow of fidelity. I've never married any of them. To date. But keep tuned for further announcements.... I'm beginning to get *that* serious about Marilyn.

Meanwhile, in the days when I was building up Playboy in the UK and switching to country weekends at Stocks, my life was quite full. Two or three days a week I'd go foxhunting. Entertaining, on the scale I enjoy takes up a lot of time. And whenever there have been extra-special ladies in my life they have shared all this with me as well as having to accept my single-man outlook.

Connie Kreski, the lady I met through Roman Polanski, had found this impossible. But Barbara Parkins, the actress star of *Peyton Place,* made fun of the whole thing. A pretty Canadian brunette, she made me laugh a lot with her mimicry and mockery. Barbara was an amusing asset at Stocks parties during her visits—memorably when, Indian-style, she would perform "rain dances." These—the reverse of what they were intended for—were satirically intended to *stop* the English rain.

Mostly my time at Stocks was limited to weekends and occasional holidays. I was making four or five trips to Chicago and Los Angeles every year for meetings with Hef and the Playboy Enterprises board.

I was very happy with my life in England. More than once Hef asked me, "Wouldn't you like to come back here, Victor?" I never felt the least inclination to do so, and told him so.

I'm not sure Hef, always so reclusive himself, ever really understood my adopted way of life. His world came to him. I had gone out to one of my own which seemed to provide everything I could possibly want.

When the oil crisis of 1973 brought wealthy Arabs to our gaming tables, business increased enormously month by month.

Hef's first visit to us in London was for the opening of the Playboy Club on Park Lane on 29 June 1966. He flew over in the "Big Bunny" and we arranged what I hoped was an enjoyable schedule for him. But I always felt it was a strain for him to be away from his mansion for long.

For me, it was a great time to remember. I had my mom over and one of our bunnies—the attractive Anthea Redfern who later married Bruce Forsythe—was dolled up in a costume made out of the Union Jack. All the girls looked fine. The Club was absolutely splendid. I felt really proud of everyone who worked for me and what we had accomplished.

Hef, as always, stayed at the Hilton. He is happier in a hotel room than as guest in a private house, even one as comfortable and well-appointed as mine. We met for several games of backgammon. As I'd more or less taught him the game, I used to take a fair amount of money off him at that time. But later, when he got good at it, I prudently suggested we lower the stakes.

Hef made another visit to London in 1971, soon after I'd bought the Clermont Club. This was a casino patronized by London's wealthiest and most distinguished gamblers. Games at the Clermont were played for stakes as high as any I had ever seen. These were the last days of swinging London, when fortunes were being made in property and other speculations.

The influx of the Arabs to London and their insistence on recycling their petrol dollars at our tables caused some unusual scenes at the Clermont Club.

One afternoon an Arab was playing roulette alone and betting several thousand pounds on each spin of the wheel. I observed that he was down well over a hundred thousand pounds.

At this point I was summoned to the reception area. A family of three Americans was at the front door asking if they could tour the premises at 44 Berkeley Square. They had a letter of introduction from one of our members.

The Clermont Club is the only surviving London townhouse designed by the mid-Georgian architect William Kent. It is a masterpiece of rococco-Georgian design.

The trio seemed pleasant enough so I assigned someone to accompany them through the premises. This was necessary because British gaming laws didn't allow visiting Americans to gamble unless they expressed the desire to do so forty-eight hours before making a casino wager.

They were entranced with the architecture. When they passed the roulette wheel where the Arab was the sole player, they stopped to watch. They seemed unfamiliar with roulette and were obviously trying to figure out the game.

After about ten minutes, they turned to leave. The Arab spoke to them. "Ever since the two of you and your beautiful daughter have stood watching me, my luck has changed. I have recovered my losses and am on the verge of winning. Could I prevail upon you to stand there for just a while longer?"

They stood for another fifteen minutes. They then started to leave, apologizing to the Arab but explaining that they had other appointments to see London architecture and a limited time in which to do it.

The Arab smiled graciously. "I understand," he said. "And I want to thank you for bringing me good luck."

He handed each of them a five-thousand pound plaque. Fifteen thousand pounds.

It was obvious to me that the Americans thought they were being given souvenirs.

"You can cash them in," I told them.

I enjoyed watching their looks of amazement when the cashier handed them thirty thousand dollars.

The Arab waved away their protestations and their thanks. "It is I who should thank you," he said with a smile.

They left the premises in shock.

We hadn't even bothered to save the letter with their names.

Another example of the kind of money that was in circulation at this time involved one of the Arab princes. He stayed at the Claridge Hotel. Whenever he was scheduled to visit us—and he was a frequent visitor—one of my assistants would go to the Claridge with a security guard to pick up a briefcase containing one hundred thousand pounds in cash. "Just enough," the prince explained, so that he and his guests could "have a good time" that evening.

Once, at 4 o'clock in the morning, he was at the Punto Banco (Baccarat) table when we announced we were about to close.

The prince discovered—almost to his chagrin—that he was a big winner. He asked one of his aides to circle the table quietly and to ask each player how much he had lost.

Losses ranged all the way up to 70,000 pounds; the bad turn-of-luck suffered by an Iranian millionaire.

When the players stood up to leave, the prince announced that he was reimbursing all the players for the amount of their losses.

Then came the startling scene. The Iranian millionaire was irate. He told the aide to the prince that he was insulted. He blustered with indignation.

The prince came over to him, put his arm around the Iranian's shoulder, and said, "Sir, if you do not accept this small gesture from me, it is quite clear that we will never become good friends."

The Iranian relented, and good friends they did indeed become.

All in all, it was a most exciting time. And, looking back, it's hard to believe I packed into it all that I did. At the office, the days were never long enough, but when I got back to the penthouse, or down to Stocks, I had enough energy left to enjoy a varied and exciting life. It's hard to single out any particularly special friends at that time, but I certainly will never forget the Collinson twins, Madeline and Mary.

They became almost permanent fixtures. And in their way they were strictly moral girls, who were very selective in their choice of boyfriends. The peculiarity about them was that neither would entertain a boyfriend whom her sister disliked.

It was not a question of dating one or the other, but both. So I had to settle for a girl on either arm whenever we went out—or stayed in—together. In case you think that was a hardship, let me tell you that those girls were among the most beautiful I have ever seen, and so identical in looks that in dim light I often mistook one for the other. They liked doing everything together. Yes, *everything*.

When I sent them over to Chicago, the twins, whose mother was Maltese and father British, made *Playboy* history by becoming the first and only Playmate double. Never before or since has Hefner approved the idea of having two girls on the centerfold in place of one.

As Hugh Hefner once remarked to my friend Richard Johnson, the actor: "Victor and I like a lot of the same things and a lot of the same girls. But there are differences. I'm always satisfied with what I've got, while Vic always wants more."

In the case of the twins, it wasn't a case of wanting more but having to settle for two-in-one or none at all. I settled. Anyway, knowing how Hef's life really was, I knew he must be joking.

Chapter Eight
TO JAWS WITH LOVE

By 1969 the British gaming operation was starting to dwarf the profits of the other Playboy divisions and making a disproportionately large contribution to the parent company's sales figures of $100 million. The Group's net profits of $7.5 million were five times what we had earned seven years ago, and before tax these earnings had risen from $2.5 million to an impressive $16.5 million.

There were warning signs of trouble ahead, but these were ignored. After all, the magazine was attracting more advertising of a high calibre than ever before. Hefner was venturing into films, records and book publishing with the confidence of a man who could make no mistakes. Even the most critical business-press reporters paid little attention to such downward indicators as the $4 million invested in movie production—*Macbeth* was to lose us $1.5 million—or the losses of two hotels in the Group, the Miami Plaza and the Playboy Towers in Chicago, to which Playboy had given a $3 million facelift.

In London, I could see that our part in the company's success story was covering more than a fair share of these losses, but I trusted Hefner to bring the other divisions of the company into profitability before long.

If the administrative extravagances bothered me, I kept that to myself.

All through the early part of the seventies, up to the first months of 1974, Playboy bounded ahead. Hef launched *Oui*, the companion magazine to *Playboy* but with greater appeal for well-travelled sophisticates and foreigners. Overseas editions of *Playboy* were launched successfully in Germany, Italy and France. A Japanese edition was planned. In America the magazine's circulation rose to more than seven million.

These promising results and new ventures were diverting attention from serious problems at the heart of the company. In 1971, our Hotels had lost $1.7 million despite previous forecasts predicting an early return to profitability. Though the fact was disguised, Playboy's Clubs and other divisions had lost their impetus. To the shrewd investors who had rushed in to oversubscribe Hefner's public flotation in November 1971—buying the shares of Playboy Enterprises, Inc., at $23.50—the stock market performance of the company was disheartening. Having risen to $25.50—its all-time highest—in early 1972, Playboy's share price fell rapidly. In a few months it was down to $14.00 before recovering to $19.00 in 1973.

Analysts, searching for reasons for the stock's weakness, blamed "embarrassment." Britain's Reuters News Agency went so far as to label the "type of magazines and clubs" as the cause of Playboy's failure to attract larger institutions and banks as investors, and though one could afford to laugh at such hidebound concepts, the shares stayed stubbornly low.

By mid-1975 I had begun to suspect that all was not well with the Chicago operation. What was wrong? Playboy never had failed to show profits in any year of its existence. But in the second quarter of 1975 there was a sudden sharp shock when reports told of a $2.7 million downturn in sales.

Hef reacted dramatically. He demoted his executive vice-president and chief operating officer, Bob Preuss, to senior vice-president group executive. And Preuss joined him in taking a 25 per cent cut in salary.

What followed was an economy drive, fierce if short-lived. Editorial meetings on the magazine had always been occasions for enjoying rich food; this was now reduced to sandwiches. Economy flights took the place of first-class. And expense sheets were savagely trimmed.

Hef himself sacrificed his own semi-annual dividend of $400,000 to find cash for the company to pay a dividend of 6 cents to all other shareholders. Without this, confidence in the company would have been dangerously sapped.

From London it all looked unreal. We were doing tremendous business. Reading Hef's statements to the press at the time, it's hard to believe that there were any problems. After all, as he said, we were experiencing renewed strength in the British casino operations and our entertainment division losses were—though he did not mention how slowly—being reduced.

Was there or was there not anything to worry about? To an extent, it seemed to me that we were suffering from a bad press, an overworked Preuss, and an envious outside world. As I told Bill Gerhauser, my assistant managing director in London, "We've had poor sales figures before without all these dismal forecasts. They're gunning for us at the moment. That's all it is."

In January, Hef suffered a sad personal blow which reflected badly on the company. Bobbi Arnstein, his executive secretary who had been with him for sixteen years, committed suicide after she was involved in drug offences. She seems to have been a party to the illegal activities of a young boyfriend. During the investigation which followed her death, Hefner and many of his top aides, his mansion guests and personal friends, were quizzed.

I had known Bobbi was upset. In 1963, shortly before I came to Britain, she had been very friendly with my young brother Tom who at that time had a promising career as an editor with *Playboy*. Their relationship had reached the point where she hoped he would one day marry her, although at the time he was still married. He was teaching her to drive his car when she spun it off the road and overturned it, killing Tom instantly. The effect on Bobbi was traumatic, and she never forgave herself. No amount of psycho-analysis, none of the sympathy given to her by all of us, could permanently heal the wound of that terrible accident.

Bobbi's conviction for supposedly helping her young boyfriend,

Ron Sharp, to ferry cocaine from Miami to Chicago was the hex. None of it had the slightest connection with Playboy, but that didn't stop the press or the politicians.

On the night of her death, Hef was aware that Bobbi's conviction on a drugs charge, awaiting hearing on appeal, was damaging the company's image. At the press conference which followed, he declared: "For the record, I have never used cocaine, or any other hard drugs or narcotics—and I am willing to swear to that fact under oath, and penalty of perjury...." At the end of a long, emotional speech, he wept. The media seemed to enjoy his distress.

James Thompson, the United States Attorney in Chicago, was involved in the state governorship fight. He ran a witch-hunt with plenty of headlines. This helped him win election as the governor of Illinois.

No Abe Lincoln he!

I got a frantic call from Bob Gutwillig, Playboy's marketing vice-president. "Victor, fly over and I'll meet you at the airport. We've got to persuade Hef to step down until this thing blows over."

A grand jury was to rule on the results of the investigation. It was true that things looked bleak.

I believed that if Hef retreated, it would give the hounds the scent of the fox. It would encourage their pursuit. If Hefner acted like a guilty person he'd be branded "guilty" whatever the evidence.

So I refused to fly to Chicago. Instead, I notified Hef. He promptly fired the unfortunate Gutwillig, who was only trying, however mistakenly, to help the company.

The timing couldn't have been worse. Combined with the downturn in Playboy's profits, the continuing decline was ominously seen as a beginning of the end of the whole Playboy structure. Hefner signed the third-quarter report alone instead of with Bob Preuss, as in the past. It made lousy reading. Sales had dropped $6 million from the previous quarter and were $3 million less than the comparable previous year's figure. Net losses totalled $387,000 or 4 cents a share.

Then I got a call from Hef asking me to come over.

I took the ordinary economy flight to Chicago, in keeping with the economy drive. Hef seemed relaxed when I met him. There were lines of pain rather than strain on his face, which I attributed to Bobbi's suicide rather than the bleak financial news. We talked about this and that, the usual chat of old friends meeting after a tragedy. Business worries were not weighing on him, so far as I could see.

Next day there was a board meeting. Hef announced that he was appointing me to take over all the Hotels and Clubs in the group. He asked me to divide my time between England and the United States so as to carry out a lot of necessary pruning. I agreed, happy to join the fray.

Some people had been fired—usually the wrong ones—and as Thomas Weyr later wrote in his book, *Reaching for Paradise,* there was "plenty of fat left untouched by the quasi-hysterical efforts undertaken in late 1974 to reduce costs by chopping blindly with a halberd."

"Do whatever is necessary," Hef told me. "You'll have a free hand. Carry an axe if you have to, and you *will* have to! I want the business brought into line."

Well, that didn't look too impossible a task. If Hef meant what he said, I should in time be able to eliminate loss-making sidelines, reduce waste and bolster profits.

"You do mean a really free hand?" I asked. Hef nodded.

So there I was, president in charge of Playboy Clubs, Hotels and Casinos throughout the world, and with a licence from Hefner to axe every loss-maker in the division. But while my new province was losing money in ways which strictly speaking concerned only its internal structure, this reflected on overall Group profits. So it seemed to me that wasteful extravagances in the parent company were equally fundamental to the spring-cleaning operation.

I made several suggestions for having these removed. Some of my recommendations were not popular with Hefner or his home-based associates, but I persisted.

Hefner was now spending nearly all his time in Los Angeles

among the movie stars. He had almost deserted Chicago. Yet the mansion and the house next door, where the boardroom was, probably only got used once a month at that. The company had to keep a sizeable regular staff on the payroll just to open the place every thirty days or so.

Another obvious extravagance was Hefner's private (but company-owned) jet, the DC9 "Big Bunny." The figures showed that for the luxury of not travelling with the hoi-poloi, Hef was spending a million and a half dollars a year. He did not use the aircraft much.

Landing and parking at a major airport cost between three and four thousand dollars. Then there was gas, maintenance, and licensing fees as well as crew salaries. It was, of all the Playboy extravagances, the most flamboyantly unnecessary.

I suggested the plane be sold. As I told my administrative colleagues: "I can lick the Hotels and Clubs into profitable shape. But to get the company on an even keel we'll have to cut out a lot of fat."

I had moved into the corner office of the seventh floor of the Playboy building, living meanwhile in an apartment in Playboy towers. For the next couple of years I spent roughly four months out of every twelve in the States. I didn't move back to America in the full sense, but I divided my time as Hef had wished. And, slowly, the ship turned around.

As I worked through the days and long into the nights, the extent of the problem at times seemed overwhelming. Arnie Morton had left the company in 1973. Others who had been brought in seemed, as I studied the figures, to have followed a disastrous path. As I told Bill during one of my many flying hops to London: "With Morton gone, the whole operation is a real mess. There are people running the divisions who couldn't run a successful hamburger joint. As a matter of fact, that is what they have turned some of the Clubs into."

Hefner depended on his highly paid executives to keep the business going. Some had failed him. As I saw it, I had to act decisively and ruthlessly. Some of the people who had been running things, or not running them, had to go.

The startling fact is that the domestic Clubs and Hotels were losing $8 million a year. To get them to a breakeven point was to take nearly five years of concentrated management. The problem was where to start.

Should I sell off some of the biggest loss-makers? Systematically, I went through them all. For a while I even considered closing Great Gorge. I tried taking the Playboy name off the Hotels, hoping that this would attract more family and convention business. It did, but the loss of revenue from Playboy members more than offset the small gain. The Playboy name went back on.

It was a suggestion from an old colleague, Tom Perine, who was our first franchisee, that finally turned the corner. "Your best hope, Victor," he told me one day, "is to put the hotels on a time-sharing concept. If you sell hotel units for fixed periods each year to different customers, this should give you the flexibility you need." I did, and it worked.

At the same time I went to work on the Clubs. People around Hefner were warning that our keyholders would complain if we closed any of the Clubs their keys entitled them to visit. "They won't stand for any reduction in the facilities they have paid for," I was told.

I said: "Close the Clubs and then worry about it."

So I went through the list and sorted out the ones that were losing the most money. Everybody in the company knew that I was on the warpath, with Hefner's full backing.

My secretary let it slip one day, almost as a joke. "You know what they are calling you? 'Jaws'!" She found it amusing even if I didn't. But the job had to be done.

The more I examined the profit and loss accounts, the clearer it became that frightening mistakes were being made. The New York Club was being remodelled, but not as we would have done it in London, floor-by-floor. The whole goddamn place had to be closed during the work. That redecoration and restructuring was setting us back $3-4 million.

All the Clubs were in a bad way. Memberships were bringing in

$5 million from a million members from their five dollar renewal fees. The bad debt figure was ridiculously high.

A child could see that the company was having its brains beaten out by use of its own credit operation. All Playboy members, until I took over, carried a Playboy credit card. What this meant was that a member could run up bills with us without endangering his credit outside. If a member used an American Express or Diners card and defaulted on payment, that would be the end of his or her credit. But with our cards, all it meant was that they had to go somewhere else to have dinner and spend the evening.

I cancelled the credit operation. No longer would we sell keys with charge privileges. In future, the key was simply to get into the Clubs. Old members with clean records still had charge privileges, but as soon as any member's account became ninety days overdue, his credit with Playboy was chopped off. We continued to honor all outside major credit cards.

So that took us out of the credit business. The next problem was to increase our hotel bookings, and especially to attract the right sort of guests. Some of the hotels were suffering because guests complained that other people using the hotel were socially undesirable. I soon learned that we'd been encouraging group bookings from social clubs and others who swamped the hotel with their members, taking over a whole bunch of rooms at cut rates for a weekend, and making other guests feel like outsiders.

Not only was this pretty crummy business, and dragging down the reputation of our hotels where it was practiced, but with the discounts given to these groups it hardly justified its existence financially. I put a stop to it.

Another area I moved into, with the help of my previous experience, was entertainment. When I took over the man in charge of booking was Sam Di Stefano. I called him in. "This is going to be tough on you," I told him, "but from now on we have to justify the cost of all the acts we book." I suggested that at Lake Geneva, Wisconsin, we should book country and western acts in order to attract more people from northern Wisconsin, Milwaukee and the mid-west. Changes like this all had positive effects.

Harder, and often personally discomforting, was the urgent need to reduce spending by top executives, some of whom were personal friends, and to fire non-essential employees. As a starter, I recommended that Hefner's mansion house staff in Chicago be reduced from fifty to twelve.

All service personnel in the Chicago Hotel and Playboy Club were subjected to cost-accounting scrutiny. In Chicago alone, we must have terminated thirty people, each with an average yearly salary of $25,000. Since staff benefits were about equal to their wages and expenses, this saved the Group a couple of million dollars a year.

I was reminded of this when, a few years later, I had the unhappy task of firing my own son. Val had spent ten years with the company. He is a friendly, easy-going guy and very much a creature of his age group. Like many of today's youngsters, he occasionally smoked marijuana. I disapproved but recognized that, as an adult, he has the right to make his own mistakes.

Val had joined the company with Hefner's blessing and risen to become resident director of the Bahamian Club at the age of thirty. I'd heard he wasn't getting along well with some of the officials in the Bahamas, including, notably, the head of the Gaming Board, Perry Christie. Officially, as president of the Clubs, I couldn't afford the risk of upsetting this potentially pofitablc gaming enterprise in the islands. So I moved Val to another job.

Dan Stone, my deputy in America, was made responsible for Val's career. I asked him: "What have we got for Val? He seems to be in the line of fire."

Stone indicated that there might be some difficulty in placing my son, for the very reason he *was* my son. "Some of the guys don't like the link he has with you, Victor," he told me. "After all, you are the boss, and they probably fear his access to you."

Val had to face up to a certain amount of hostility. Then he made an unfortunate mistake. The night before he left the Bahamas (for discussions with Stone about a transfer), Val was asked by a girlfriend, one of our Chicago bunnies, to bring her a "couple of joints" when he flew over. Like an idiot, he put a few in his pocket.

In the meantime, someone had alerted US Customs. They were waiting for him. He was arrested for possession of drugs. He was fined. He did everything to prevent his connection with Playboy coming out.

It wasn't a big deal, and ordinarily a large company might have overlooked it in the case of a trusted young executive. But for a sensitive Playboy, still smarting from the rumors and allegations connected to Bobbi Arnstein's suicide, the matter was grave. The very idea that a Club manager would do such a thing was unforgivable.

In November 1980, feeling a little of what Irish Judge Lynch must have felt when sentencing his own son to be hanged, I fired my son Val. He understood the decision—and maybe the pain that went with it.

Back in 1975 when, like it or not, I had to snap my "jaws" wherever deadwood showed, the big thing was to close down the turkeys—the Clubs not making money. At the same time, prestige and morale depended on us holding up our corporate image. For this, I had to exclude our flagship Clubs in Chicago, Los Angeles and New York. They were musts, while every other one of our Clubs had to be considered strictly on its merits.

If there weren't enough people using any of the other Clubs and spending sufficient money to make them profitable, then they weren't going to be missed. I closed San Francisco. To the staff there it was a terrible blow, but the fact was that the members weren't upset. They still had Playboy key facilities in all other centers we operated.

I closed Kansas City. The St. Louis Club was a franchise but located in a part of town that was steadily becoming a slum. After discussions with the franchise owners, they agreed to move the Club to the suburbs where business picked up immediately.

Conversely, the Atlanta Club moved and was doing worse than before. I urged the franchisers to close it down. All these changes went through without a word of protest from Hefner. But when I saw that our hotel in Jamaica could be sold for a good price, he made it clear he wanted to hang on to it. I told him, "If we don't sell now the price could drop severely."

Violence was spreading in Kingston and Montego Bay under the Manley government. Hef agreed that could have bleak consequences. With the news coverage the violence was receiving in America, it was obvious that American tourism would evaporate. Nevertheless, Hef said he wanted to hang on to the Jamaica Playboy at least for the time being.

I closed it down. We leased it for a couple of years. Now it's abandoned and a problem for the company. Another rabbit had become a white elephant.

Meanwhile, I was dealing with still more of the Clubs. Montreal was losing money, so I shut that down. One trouble with many of the Clubs was that they were nearly twenty years old. Districts had changed, and in Montreal the place had originally been built in the early sixties, in what was then a popular downtown urban area. Now the area had become dangerous to walk through at night.

Some of my colleagues probably thought I was crazy not to reopen in a better part of town. But these Clubs cost at least one million dollars each to equip and launch. In hard times I couldn't afford to be foolhardy.

I claim no responsibility for the way Playboy rid itself of some of the best and most loyal executives they had. As some observers noted, Robert Preuss was the "fall guy." Bob was not himself fired, but through a series of successive demotions he was moved further and further from the center of power.

He'd joined Hefner without title or full authority, to take on the responsible role of executive vice-president of Playboy Enterprises, Inc. When he stepped down, he humbly admitted that Playboy's explosive growth had overwhelmed him. Maybe so. But some would say that Bob Preuss had been given too much responsibility early on and too much blame when the castle began to crumble.

Was Hefner himself blameless? One of his executive assistants, Dick Rosenzweig, said later: "Hefner was so involved in writing the philosophy that he was not accessible to anyone for making decisions." Press reports, accusing Hef of stepping aside from responsible running of the company, made no bones about his detachment. He himself summed it up. "Other people have been running the company for a long time. I'll make major decisions. For example, I'll decide which particular island this ship will go to next. Yes, I'll make that decision, but getting there is up to the captain and the crew."

On 13 April 1976 the crunch came. The influential *Wall Street Journal* front-paged Hefner's continuing problems under the headline "Playboy's Slide." Hef was quoted as seeing brighter days ahead, and I was singled out as his saving champion.

The *Journal's* reporters had interviewed several of the top people who had business dealings with Playboy. According to them, Playboy's "days of booming growth" had come to a permanent stop. Competition from publisher Bob Guccione with his magazine *Penthouse* was, in the *Journal's* eyes, causing *Playboy* to become "a little frayed." The damaging report concluded: "For years the transfusion—*Playboy* magazine's profits—has kept it alive but now that is diminishing too. Without radical surgery, the life of the body is in danger."

Hammer blows of this kind are inevitable in any big corporation faced with recession. This one certainly didn't make my task any easier. Hotels had lost $14.4 million at this point. The occupancy rate in all four of them—Lake Geneva, The Towers, Jamaica and Great Gorge—had fallen below 60 per cent by the end of our financial year in June 1975. Some fell even lower. But the *Journal* was wrong in one particular: "Sceptics doubt that [my economy drive] will restore Playboy to its imperial grandeur." I had every confidence it would. In the spring of 1976 Hef's "Big Bunny" was sold for $4 million—more than its book value. Advertising in the magazine perked up, due to a rate reduction. Playboy's third-quarter report showed profits after three consecutive losses, and continued to show a profit for the next two. Playboy Enterprises were once again climbing the mountain.

But that spring was significant in other ways, too. A senior newsman, Derick January Daniels, was recruited to Playboy's top management from his presidential chair of the Knight-Ridder newspapers. Daniels, a shrewd self-confident manager, assumed control of the company. Playboy announced his appointment as president, as of 4 October. His salary: $250,000 plus heavy corporate perks and a five-year contract.

Since I had deliberately avoided seeking any major salary increase myself during the company's economy drive, I decided that this appointment put me in danger of falling behind. Daniels did not seem to me to be someone more capable than I was, so when Hefner asked my opinion of him before hiring him and, after lunching him at the University Club in Chicago, I reported that I was not terribly impressed. As I had explained to Hef, Daniels did not seem to me to be the kind of guy who would be any trouble to us, but I did not see him as being any great asset to the business.

Now here was a new man, coming in from outside, being given a contract which I lacked and with a lot more money than I was getting, while my end of the business was providing most of Playboy's profits. Largely as an ego booster, I asked Hefner to give me what I thought I was worth.

At the same time, to make the point as strongly as possible, I said I would resign if there was any reluctance to agree to my demand. I said: "Look, if you don't want to give me a lot of money, I'll quit. I'll go form my own casino chain operation."

The answer was prompt and favorable. My salary of $100,000 was doubled. I was given a three-year contract—which was just as well, in view of what was to come. When finally I was fired, I at least had the satisfaction of knowing that I would receive half pay for three years. Half of everything, including bonus, which in total amounted to more than my full basic wage.

But a lot of people thought I was gunning for the job Daniels had. That wasn't true for several reasons. Chief among them was the fact that I had no wish to leave England, and I wouldn't have left

England. I was happy there. I also saw a certain advantage in running the American Clubs and Hotels from there, because I figured that while we were running them under the British umbrella, our losses outside the UK could be set against our tremendous British profits (under what is known as "group relief" in taxation terms).

If it ever occurred to me that I might be attracting envy as well as relief and gratitude from my distant colleagues in Chicago and Los Angeles, I dismissed the notion. In view of what was to happen, I should have paid more attention to this very human characteristic.

All in all, I think Hef himself appreciated my reign as the cost-cutting head of all the Playboy Clubs. Out of a clear blue sky a package arrived on my desk in Chicago one day in 1977. It contained a mounted set of shark's teeth on a trophy board; underneath was an engraved brass plate: "To Jaws with love from Hef and Barbie."

Above left My mother's 75th birthday party was held at Stocks in June 1980. *Above right* Daughter Meredith and grandson Kyle at Lake Geneva Playboy Club, Wisconsin. *Below* A snapshot of Val (Victor Aubrey Lownes IV) with female admirers.

With Marilyn Cole at Stocks in 1977—just before our split-up; and (*below*) in November 1981—after our reunion.

Above The Madhatter's Handicap at Plumpton races, March 1980; Prince Charles (*right*) later overtook me. We both finished second—he second from first, me second from last. *Below* With **Marilyn Cole**. *Below right* Silvana Suarez from Argentina—the reigning Miss World—showed no objection to posing with me at Los Angeles airport in June 1979. Later she was less keen.

Playboy's 25th birthday party, celebrated at Stocks on July 4, 1979. Three thousand attended.

Above left Peter Beard with Caroline Kennedy and Caroline Black at Stocks (with paintings of Peter by Francis Bacon). *Above right* Christie Hefner, Hugh's daughter, with Frank Oz, at Stocks. *Below* Celebrities at the Playboy 25th birthday party, 1979: from left, daughter Cynthia Cleese looking over the shoulder of John Cleese, Victor Lownes, Bernie Winters, Marilyn Cole, Richard Johnson, Reggie Bosanquet and Lance Percival.

Above My last project for Playboy. I never saw the Atlantic City building finished—it opened a few days after I was dismissed. *Below* At a cabaret held in her honor at the Whitney Museum, New York, in January 1981, Mabel Mercer—the singer who played such a big part in my original meeting with Hefner—shared a table with Debbie Chenoweth (*left*) and me.

"I gather they're still not allowed to go out with the customers." (Reproduced by permission of Express Newspapers)

Above Jak's cartoon in the *New Standard* greeted Trident's take-over of the Playboy-owned clubs in London. Trident announced that they were going to do away with the Bunny costume and introduce a new one. Dulcie, my pet monkey, was very honored. *Below* My single remaining share of stock in Playboy, which I have kept as a souvenir. At one time I was the second largest stockholder. Derick Daniels, whose signature appears on the left, 'resigned' recently. He was replaced by Christie Hefner.

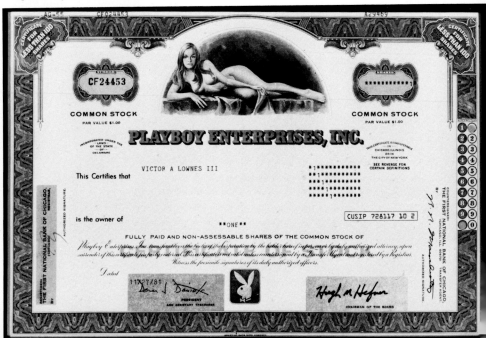

Chapter Nine
VALUE VERIFIED, VISION VINDICATED

Meanwhile, development of our British Playboy empire was involving me in a number of deals. After I'd added the Clermont Club to our casino operation in London in 1970, I risked putting bunnies and gaming into the English provinces. We opened Clubs in Manchester and Portsmouth/Southsea. Though my "Jaws" activity took me away a lot, I still managed to see to it that the Clubs were well run and that profits in our English group continued to grow. Indeed, I was widely quoted as saying that some of our Arab gamblers would cheerfully wager $200,000 "without folding a single tent," and this was no exaggeration. Between January 1976 and June 1981 our UK casinos turned over a staggering billion three hundred and twenty million dollars!

In 1979, I decided the profits could be extended still further. The Victoria Sporting Club was for sale. Although it had been raided by the police under its previous owners and faced a battle against loss of its gaming licence, I felt confident enough to bid for it against sizeable opposition put up by cinema and property tycoon Laurie Marsh and ex-Mecca boss Eric Morley. My offer of twelve million dollars was finally accepted, though in Chicago I gathered that the risk I was taking was viewed with rather less than hearty enthusiasm.

I had been instrumental in forming and was serving as a director of the British Casino Association, to support and further the aims and business of those of us who ran successful, lawful gaming. It was at a meeting of the Association in May 1979, in the Curzon House Club, that Cyril Stein of Ladbroke's opened my eyes to the dangerously corrupt methods of some of our competitors.

Stein knew that I had reason to believe that his people were bribing porters of West End hotels to bring guests to his casinos. Also he and his minions had been noting the car registration numbers of guests at other casinos. Through barefaced bribery of the police (paying 50p per number to the operator of the police computer in Nottingham for the names and addresses of the owners), they were then telephoning these people and offering them dinner, sending them flowers, and inviting them to Ladbroke's casinos in the West End of London.

Before the meeting, I had already put Ladbroke on notice that we were going to file objections to all their illegal acts.

Ladbroke were doing these things to us at Playboy and the Clermont, and, according to the press, gathering information about us in this underhand and illegal way. I felt that for me *not* to protest was another way of saying: "Oh, well. We're all doing it." So I insisted on standing up and being counted.

If Cyril Stein had behaved differently at the meeting you wouldn't now be reading this book. Our beginnings never know our ends. Instead of condemning what his people were doing and assuring me they'd stop, he threatened me. Only after that did I bring in Playboy's lawyers and get really involved.

Stein made a statement which directly challenged everything I stood for. He wanted, he said, to draw the Association's notice to the fact that Playboy was objecting to renewal of his licences. His words were: "I'd like to say that if Playboy doesn't withdraw its objections, the mud's really going to fly. And it's not just going to be at Playboy!"

The personal threat against me was one which everyone at the table recognized. Far too clever directly to oppose what we all sought (a spring-cleaning of the entire business by ourselves), he was using his strength, as one of Britain's largest gaming and betting controllers, to enforce a cover-up.

I remember thinking that there was an unsavory similarity here with Watergate. If we buckled under his threat, we—the top men in the industry—would be meekly accepting Stein's threat against disclosure. Yet Playboy certainly had nothing to hide. The more I thought about it, the angrier I became.

I was sitting next to Eddie Thomas of Pleasurama, a man I knew and respected. If it was going to come to a shooting match, I felt sure he could be relied on to back me up. I scribbled on a piece of paper: "He's trying to get you chaps to pressure me into withdrawing my objections."

Eddie took the note and read it. He raised his eyes to mine and nodded his head in agreement. I took another piece of paper, and wrote: "Fuck 'em," and passed it over to Eddie. Again he nodded his head, this time more vigorously.

For the rest of the meeting Stein avoided the subject. We were concerned with new forms of taxation of casinos. Tax officials were recommending and Parliament was supporting a tax on profits rather than the existing tax on the number of tables. Under the existing system clubs with customers risking only a few pounds were paying as much as those, like our own, seeing an average $8,000 a head from each player.

Stein was against disclosing any figures. My own feelings were the exact opposite. I not only backed the reform efforts, but I'd been working up support for the Gaming Board in its clean-up attempts by refusing licenses to doubtful operators.

Indeed, I was strongly in favor of us banding together to present a united front to Parliament. I'd even hired a PR firm with lobbying experience to push for our cause.

But Cyril Stein would not support any of this. It seemed he didn't want to co-operate with the reformers. Perhaps he couldn't see the writing on the wall. And no doubt he thought we were all crazy to go charging off to the Inland Revenue with all kinds of facts and figures which, he maintained, would only bring increased taxation on us.

To me, it was a fact of life which we had to live with, nor did it seem unreasonable. One of the reasons why I was then negotiating to buy the lucrative Victoria Sporting Club and its betting shops was that I felt sure we were going to need increased earnings to pay for the rise in taxes which those changes could bring.

And at Playboy and the Clermont (as well as in our provincial Clubs) I was confident we were acting within both the letter and the spirit of the law. Any London casinos stepping deliberately out of line could only damage us all.

My time at the meeting was limited. I had already announced that I had to leave early, because I had an urgent problem on my hands in Portsmouth. So towards the end of the afternoon I scooped up my papers and prepared to leave. That was when Cyril Stein repeated his threat.

It would cost him his casinos.

Some time earlier I had asked Alex Alexander, the then retired head of Ladbroke gaming, how true the reports of Ladbroke's illegal activities were. "Are you doing this?" I'd asked. "Are you *really* sending people to snoop on cars outside Playboy and other clubs?"

He had categorically denied it. "Don't believe everything you read in *Private Eye,*" he told me. "It's not true at all."

I suppose if Alex had not retired when he did, soon after that conversation, things might have ended differently. I doubt he would have directly threatened us as Stein did.

Certainly, if Stein had come to me and said: "Here's a list of people who became members of Ladbroke because of our approach to them, after they were seen to have been visiting Playboy or the Clermont; we are going to write them letters and straighten things out"—the whole unpleasant business would have ended then and there.

But he hadn't done that. And the meeting where he threatened me, and tried to coerce the whole industry, was a battleground of his choosing. If I must look back on it now as the battle I won which later lost me the war, so be it.

When I returned from Portsmouth I telephoned Group Captain Steve Stephens, Secretary of the British Casino Association, and went over the whole matter with him. His sympathetic ear added to my determination to go through with lodging a complaint against Ladbroke. Instinct then prompted me to double-check our own operation.

I went to Gerhauser; to our head of gaming Bernard Mulhearn; to our credit controller Andy Wheeler; and to our financial director John Wintle. I asked each the same question: "Do you feel that any adverse capital could be made out of any practices, past or present, that we have engaged in?" In each case I received the same reassurance: "Absolutely not. We're one hundred percent clean."

It could be argued that there are areas—gray areas—in which interpretation of the Gaming Act leads to borderline questions. For instance, there is nothing in the Act itself which requires a casino to verify the existence of a customer's account at a bank before accepting a check from him. It is good business practice to do so, but impossible in every case when dealing with foreigners on short visits to the UK. In the end, it has to become a judgment decision by management. On the spot and at the time. Since Playboy's bad debts in Britain were less than three per cent of turnover, I would say that our judgment wasn't too bad.

The Act does clearly say, however, that checks, once accepted, must be passed to the bank for clearance *within two banking days* and never on any account returned to the customer. This we did without fail. And it was certainly not our policy to accept a check from a player *knowingly* if he had no account at that bank. To do so would have given the player a chance to win from us while we would have no chance of collecting if he lost.

In fact, when the allegation of a "no account" scheme being operated at our Clubs arose in February 1981 we audited all of our credit transactions. We found that, of more than 35,000 on record, only thirty-seven of the cards kept contained entries of returned checks. Only three had more than one entry to show that the person on our staff who had accepted the check should have been more careful. Yet, when the new regime took over from us they never challenged the assertion made in evidence against us that "the Casino must have known" that "no account checks" had been accepted—as if it were a common practice. Far from it.

Any multiple entries on the cards were there because checks from a foreign country could sometimes take anywhere from three weeks to three months to clear.

So the Act put the casino at a considerable disadvantage when customers included, as did ours, wealthy high rollers from far-distant lands. Because if such a player chose to do so he could stop his check and walk away with his winnings. For us to collect money by law in Middle-Eastern and Far-Eastern countries was almost impossible.

In the vast majority of cases our foreign customers were honest. It was simply hard for some of them to understand why, when they had no shortage of funds in their own banks, money they unexpectedly needed to play with could not be made available on their signature.

What was later held against us ran on from there. Let's say a big player, perhaps a member of the Royal Family of one of the oil-rich Gulf States, paid his account by check and it turned out that he had no account at the bank the check was drawn on. What would we do? Well, we would never knowingly have accepted the check in the first place, as I have said. But suppose he returned on the following day with an amount of cash equal to the sum of the check, and *then* told us that his check was no good. Under the law, we were guilty for having accepted it.

Okay, he—not ourselves—had contravened Section 16 of the Act prohibiting the extension of credit to gamblers. But we had innocently deposited the dud check for collection, as required by law. So technically we were guilty of a violation of the Gaming Act. The whole thing became nonsense.

If a man's money is supposed to be in a bank in, say, Saudi Arabia or Thailand, collection of a check can take several months. Isn't that in itself a legal extension of credit? And an even greater one than a bad check, taken on a non-existent bank account, made good the following morning?

If we found difficulty in seeing our way through the quagmire of such rules, we were not alone. The Gaming Board went before a Royal Commission to seek Parliament's clarification of that very point; indeed of the whole of that section of the Gaming Act.

So why worry? With the exciting prospect of bringing the Victoria Sporting Club under our wing, and with our profits now three times as high as any other division of the Playboy empire, there seemed no cause for alarm.

I took it as normal procedure that police had raided the Victoria Sporting Club late the previous year, and that a careful watch was being kept on many of London's busiest casinos. This was understandable in an industry where 55 per cent of Ladbroke's profits came from its casinos and 33 per cent of Coral's, not to mention our own which sometimes had exceeded 100 per cent (i.e. putting more into the parent company, Playboy Enterprises, Inc., than reached the bottom line as profit).

But, had I known it, a series of interconnected alarm bells were ringing in official ears. Soon after I had completed the purchase of the company owning the Victoria Sporting Club and its betting shops, 400 police raided Coral's, eventually costing them the right to operate casinos. This dried up the major cash flow of that company.

Cyril Stein was a bad enemy to have made. Bill Gerhauser sensed it and told me: "There's something in the wind I don't like, Victor." I told him not to be paranoid.

Playboy's financial results were to be published at the end of our fiscal year, 30 June 1980. I knew we'd still be bringing home more bacon than the whole of the rest of the Playboy empire. In 1979, I had managed to cut losses from the Clubs and Hotels outside of England to under half a million dollars. The assurances I had from my staff were like a sword in my hand. If we were clean, how could anyone hurt us?

But Bill Gerhauser had his ear to the ground in Chicago and Los Angeles, as well as London. He realized that our very success was a potential threat. Hefner's counsellors were men like Derick Daniels and Marv Huston, the financial director, both of whom were fairly new to the company.

Frank DiPrima was Hef's top legal ace, but a man of such free-ranging personal habits that I rarely invited him to Stocks during his British visits. On a memorable occasion when I had, DiPrima—or as I came to nickname him after the fiasco of my firing, "Frank De Schema"—had mistakenly wandered into a number of guest bed-rooms, several girls' rooms, and, very mistakenly, the bedroom of a startled Peter Cook. Even allowing for jet-lag and the potency of my wine cellar, this was not the sort of behavior I expected from a house guest.

He and others were running things at Playboy with, as far as I could gather, very little interference from Hefner. Their own failure to raise profits in areas which needed effective management was a constant irritation to these yoyos.

In the spring of 1980 I went on television in a major program produced by Thames TV, in which the recent raids, the Ladbroke hearings, the Coral's situation, and our own successful purchase of the Victoria Sporting Club for twelve million dollars, were discussed. Could we hope to retain our licences, and to win back, on appeal, the licence for the Victoria which had been lost as a result of the previous year's raid? I was confident we could, and said so.

If there were clouds on the horizon, they reflected a downturn in the number of Arab high rollers using our casinos. Petrodollars were flowing a little less freely than hitherto.

That summer Derick Daniels asked if I would give up the running of the US Hotels and Clubs and I told him, "Only when we have won the right to operate our casino in Atlantic City."

Had I stayed on, and if Playboy had not muddied the water so desperately with the New Jersey State Authorities, that would have been a lucrative division.

I recall the behavior of Playboy's observers at my successful appeal hearing for retention of our Victoria Sporting Club gaming licence on 14 October. It is a day I remember with considerable pride, but also with mixed feelings (in view of his later involvement in my dismissal) towards our English barrister, Gavin Lightman.

Lightman's handling of our appeal on that day was in every way admirable. He is a brilliant advocate though he seems to lack insight into people's strengths and weaknesses—even his own. As an amusing example, he has named his two delightful daughters, Sarah and Esther. But in neither case can he—due to a lisp—pronounce these names correctly. To him they are 'Tharah' and 'Ethter' and always will be.

He is not someone I would want to have running my business. But in open court he is a formidable lawyer skilled in all points of the law and in the arts of argument.

After the case, I congratulated him heartily. He had won against serious objections and in a hearing conducted by Judge Friend, who, in the eyes of many would-be licensees, is curiously misnamed.

I was in high spirits as I walked away with the licence in my pocket. I couldn't help smiling at the sad faces of two observers, Jerry Goldberg and Jim Radtke, sent over from Chicago Playboy. The looked distressed. It was almost as if they, or their masters, had been banking on my losing. Had I lost, I have no doubt now that I'd have been sacked right there and then.

As it was, I couldn't resist a touch of euphoria. "Cheer up, fellas," I said as we met coming out of the building. "We did *win* the case, you know." Their phony smiles disappeared as they climbed into a cab and returned to America.

However, this did make me think. Was I such an object of envy and mistrust that some of the guys around Hefner wanted my head? Did they really believe they could improve on the way I was handling things in London? It was a sobering thought that, had I lost the Victoria appeal, not only would my job and half a million dollars a year in salary and bonus have gone out of the window but, even if I was personally retained, Stocks would probably have had to go as well.

The house was partially owned by Playboy and, since it was being used as a bunny training center, the company was paying 90 per cent of its running costs.

Bill Gerhauser added to the gloom when he told me he'd found some notes of a meeting between Marv Huston, Derick Daniels and Don Parker in which it was suggested that I should be taken off the board of Playboy Enterprises and that Dan Stone, who ran the American Hotels and Clubs for me, should also be shoved aside— which meant out. I had stood up for Stone when Daniels had wanted to fire him earlier on, and I suspected the Chicago "Brains Trust" still had him on their hit list. But I believed my position was secure.

Meanwhile, I wasn't going to let any of these dismal rumbles spoil my elation. I fired off a cable to Hef: VICTORIA VICTORIOUS, VISION VINDICATED, VALUE VERIFIED, VERILY VICTOR.

He wrote me a warm letter of appreciation by return. From where I *thought* I was standing—with this golden break under our belts— we seemed set to double our profits at least in the time ahead.

But for me the time ahead was a bare six months.

Christmas came and went as happily as any I remember. At Ascot the previous year, 1979, wearing the "full fig" of a guest of the Royal Enclosure—grey topper, tailcoat and spats—I had met an enchanting girl, Debbie Chenoweth, and flown her back in my helicopter to Stocks, after a champagne party given by Fleet Street columnist Nigel Dempster. We'd landed on the lawn in front of the old house, having become very good friends indeed during the flight. My only concern was that my current girlfriend, Silvana Suarez, the reigning Miss World, would let her Latin temperament (Silvana is from Argentina) diminish our pleasure.

I need not have worried. The two girls took to each other, and because Silvana was always pressing me to keep a safe distance from her in public, Debbie fell into the role of chaperone. If it hadn't amused me, I might have thought the whole situation rather weird.

Still, if the girls wanted to act out their little charade I had no objection. And we in England celebrated Playboy's 25th Anniversary as a magazine and an empire. I threw a gigantic party at Stocks to mark the occasion.

Debbie had told me she had nothing against Silvana and myself enjoying each other's company, but all the publicity and the celebrity guests may have upset Silvana. Shortly beforehand, she announced in her fiery way: "You must zee to it, Veector, that zeese photographers do not snap us together." This was a bit much in view of the two months we'd been together, and I had to tell my beautiful guest that, if that was how she felt, it would be better if she didn't come to the party at all.

Apparently, you don't say such a thing to an extremely desirable, and greatly desired, Latin lady. Silvana tossed her pretty head, turned on her heel and went upstairs to pack. What she hadn't objected to in California, when we'd been there together—being seen in newspaper pictures with me—had become too much for her in England. By the time the party began she was halfway home.

So Debbie no longer had to pretend to be my, or anybody else's, chaperone, though I must say she'd made a very enchanting one. (Especially when the three of us had flown in to London Airport together, and she had primly given newspaper reporters the story of her "chaperonage." They swallowed it whole!) She was still at Stocks a year and a half later when we celebrated what was to be my last Christmas as Playboy's leading playboy in Britain.

Meanwhile Cyril Stein had lost his appeal. His casinos were no longer operating. It was a severe blow to his company, despite their far larger interest in bookmaking. How much he blamed me for the disaster I couldn't say, and at that time I had no idea he was actively working to make his threat good. Two men who had been employed by Playboy were each paid $10,000 by Ladbroke's to dig up irregularities in our operation.

In particular Stein wanted evidence that we gave porters of the big London hotels free memberships and other incentives in return for introducing guests from their hotels to our casinos.

In fact, there were no other incentives. But faced with other casinos offering bribes, and even paying commissions, to bring in business, our people felt we had to do something to protect ourselves. So we offered honorary memberships, which were perfectly legal—but only if the guests introduced were genuine friends and not paying guests at hotels where the honorary member worked.

In early 1977, when I heard that this was going on, I stopped it. It seemed to me that the arrangement could so easily be abused or misunderstood. We let them keep their free membership, but I instructed "No guests at all for these people" from then on.

Stein's payments to our ex-employees were therefore a sheer waste of $20,000. His informants told him: "This is all Playboy did. They never paid a commission." I had already made this clear on television a whole year before the objections to our licences. If the authorities had doubted us then, they could have refused our licence renewals in 1980, but they didn't. This was one reason why I felt confident of winning a fight against the objections—including one about the honorary memberships—when they were finally brought against us.

So this was how things stood as I celebrated the New Year of 1981. As I and a few close friends raised our glasses to "success in the New Year," how could any of us know what a hollow ring that wish held? Yet, five weeks later on 5 February I suffered the first of a series of devastating blows, both physical and mental, such as I would never have thought possible.

The weather was icy but I'd ridden to hounds in far worse. Prairie, my 17-hand 3-inch bay gelding, was an experienced mount, normally sure-footed. In his defense I must say that he was probably tired out when I felt him slip on a patch of ice under me. It was mid-afternoon, and I was on the point of changing horses to give him a well-earned rest.

Instead, he gave *me* one—though how well-earned I wouldn't like to say. Prairie slipped sideways and my last memory is of deliberately pitching myself in the other direction to avoid his bulk rolling on me. That was Thursday afternoon. The next thing I knew, it was Sunday.

A broken head can vary in degree. Some hairline cracks leave little more than momentary concussion. Others inflict permanent damage. Mine was bad enough to sever the nerve cord controlling my sense of smell and, to a lesser extent, taste. Apart from that, a nasty shaking, and a temporary loss of some faculties (I see from my diary how strangely distorted my writing became at that time), I was not too badly hurt. But one takes a while to recover from such injuries, and there are inevitable repercussions.

On February 20, while I was still lying in the hospital, the police raided the Clermont and Playboy Clubs. When I got back to the office I learned that a number of our files had been seized and taken away, and my staff interviewed. In my convalescent state I had to leave quite a bit of the clearing up to others.

I told Bill Gerhauser who had been acting managing director in my absence, "They probably just want to show that they're on the ball with all the clubs."

I embarked for Los Angeles to attend a meeting of Playboy Enterprises concerning the Atlantic City application. I had no notion that, back in London, a rough draft of serious objections to our licences was already being typed out in triplicate on Metropolitan Police machines.

Chapter Ten

DANIELS IN THE LOWNES DEN

The first realization that Playboy's home base was disturbed by events in London reached me in Los Angeles, six weeks after the hunting accident. My head was knitting together well.

I'd been summoned to the routine meeting of the parent company where a lot of the talk was gloomy in view of the continuing less-than-glamorous performance of most of the divisions and the still escalating costs of promotion and administration expenses.

In my slightly befuddled state it seemed to me that I'd travelled 8,000 miles to hear a bunch of "yes men" approve one more unnecessary expenditure. Hugh Hefner was being advised that in the future he ought to travel in a bullet-proof limousine. This would cost the company around $300,000. My view—and I made it plain to Daniels, DiPrima and the others—was that this would increase his target-attraction. If anyone was crazy enough to want to shoot Hef, they'd be all the more interested in doing so if they heard that he was recognized, even by his own associates in the company, as a likely target. Hefner abstained from voting on this issue, chuckled and said that if the word did leak out, he'd send the limousine to me in England.

Nevertheless, the directors nodded agreement. Since they had managed to maintain the company's administrative costs at $18.5

million for a further year *only* by sliding $1.8 million on to the Club and Hotel division (slyly covered in a small-print footnote in the 1981 Annual Report), they probably felt free to spend the stockholders' money. I didn't. And even more I didn't feel that it was advisable to place Hefner at additional risk.

Just two weeks before this, the police raid on Playboy in London had gravely unnerved my Chicago-based associates. In the States a "raid" is a far more serious affair, and they probably visualized our Clubs being ransacked and document cabinets broken into. It wasn't like that at all, and I had no fears about the consequences.

Before I left that March 23 meeting, I announced that it seemed a waste of time for me to come all that way to be the only one voting against the company's latest extravagance. Especially since I knew they were going to buy the $300,000 limousine—which of course they did.

Word had reached the New Jersey licensing authorities that Playboy-London was in trouble. Since they were hearing Playboy's application for a gaming licence of their Atlantic City Casino—in the association formed with Elsinore (a public company controlled by billionaire financier Jay Pritzker)—this was a matter of some considerable consequence.

My associates told me that my connection with the licence application in America could prove an embarrassment. Indeed, the New Jersey people had asked that those of us involved with the London licences—Bill Gerhauser, Chris Rafael, Bernie Mulhearn, and myself—should step out of the picture at least until matters were settled. This sounded crazy to me. What reason had we to hide?

My reluctance was mainly due to my belief that the whole London problem was nothing more than smoke. No charges had been made against any of us in London, and my belief that we were being attacked to demonstrate that we were no different from other casino operators remained unchallenged.

Nevertheless we agreed to step down temporarily. Ironically, this was almost exactly one year before Hefner was faced with having to do the same thing, only permanently—on the recommendation of the same New Jersey authorities.

I flew out of Los Angeles convinced that I had done all I could to help the company, even though I somewhat resented the unnecessary waste of my time.

Not until I read the report of the later hearing after Playboy-London licences had been officially refused did I fully realize the slow, torturous involvement of the police and of Stein's Ladbroke organization.

I fully appreciated the strength of our position. Had I been allowed to do so, I felt confident of reversing the decision on appeal.

As Playboy's leading counsel, Mr. Robert Alexander, QC, had said at the hearing: "Over a period of a decade there has been no suggestion of dishonesty or corruption of staff, no suggestion of cheating . . .

"Our rival, Ladbroke, had paid informers," Mr. Alexander said, "as an act of retaliation," because I had told the Gaming Board of their irregularities. He also made it indelibly clear that "for some reason Mr. Stein's Ladbroke did not think it was in the public's interest that bribery and corruption should be exposed, and sought revenge.

"What this inquiry has revealed was how differently affairs were conducted at Playboy. Playboy kept full accounts and cooperated fully with the investigating authorities."

As indeed we did, in all innocence. Only when one of Playboy's attorneys told me, after the case, of efforts by a former Playboy executive to damage us, did I begin to appreciate the web of intrigue which our success had generated and the damage which could be wreaked by a disgruntled former employee or someone paid to condemn us by an even more disgruntled former competitor.

Less than two weeks after the LA board meeting I was in another plane heading the other way. Playboy's property in Nassau, Bahamas, had never been profitable and a lot of money—some of it my own—was tied up in it. The situation had become inflamed by fears that the wrong decisions could further damage our chances of gaining the Atlantic City licence.

Playboy's casino operation in Nassau had an unfortunate history. Originally we'd been introduced to the Prime Minister, Linden O.

Pindling, by the art-dealer Frank Lloyd of London's Marlborough
Galleries. I had bought several paintings from Lloyd, including two
by Francis Bacon. He was a respected member of London's cultural
life prior to his connection with the notorious Mark Rothko scandal,
in which he was found guilty of acting improperly as trustee of the
artist's estate.

But our dealings in the Bahamas had not proved fruitful. Firstly,
the casino we were licensed to operate was dwarfed by the islands'
much more glamorous main gaming operation. Secondly, we were
obstinately limited in our right to advertise our casino's location,
which was slightly off the beaten track.

The casino was *losing* half a million dollars a year. I was
determined to correct this; if necessary, by selling the place unless I
could get a substantial reduction in the rent and/or the taxes
(amounting to about $3 million a year).

My Chicago associates were terrified, apparently, that the New
Jersey authorities would use any retreat as yet another sign of
Playboy's inability to operate a profitable, harmonious casino.

As we discussed it, I realized that this and the Atlantic City
interest I held had both taken on an unhealthy color in their minds.
Although I discounted any possible threat which may have been
posed by the police raid in London, they saw things differently.

The situation became even more acute by the static coming from
Playboy's partner in the $135-150 million Atlantic City Hotel and
Casino project. The joint Playboy-Elsinore company directors were
getting nervous over the strict form of inquisition-like inquiry being
conducted by the New Jersey authorities.

Again, I was pressed to leave the picture. I personally owned 15
per cent of the Nassau operation and my deputy managing director,
Bill Gerhauser, had 10 per cent. In Atlantic City, I was already in for
$1.6 million. But with costs escalating from the original estimate of
only $80 million I was getting nervous. How much more would the
venture cost me, should we fail to get the license?

Having established that Bill was willing to sell out his end, I jumped at the board's offer of $2.2 million (which was virtually my entire investment) for my interest in both the Bahamas and Atlantic City. I personally felt that Playboy would have done much better to have closed the Bahamas Casino down—which would have cost me money—and got rid of a losing situation, but they chose not to do that.

When I flew back to Florida, to spend a few days with my mother, I was in a daze. I don't suppose it helped that I still wasn't a hundred per cent fit. It upset me that my colleagues had been so insistent on my stepping aside when I was the only one among them with first-hand experience of running a successful gaming operation.

On Friday, April 10, I was back in London—and met with the disconcerting news that the police and the Gaming Board were to object to the renewal of licenses for the Playboy Casino and the Clermont Club.

A hearing was set for the middle of September at Caxton Hall. Any objections to the Victoria Sporting Club and our provincial clubs in Portsmouth and Manchester were to be heard later. I studied the charges and was convinced that they were technicalities.

Chiefly, they came under six heads: our acceptance of "no account" checks, the acceptance of the checks from people who had previously given us checks which had been dishonored; the practice of certain players making "call bets" (no money down bets); honorary membership for hotel porters; the questionable behavior of my friend Abdul Khawaja; and the personal gambling of one of our directors, Clement Freud.

As regards the checks, the head of the Gaming Board, Lord Allen, had told me more than once that the Act was "anything but crystal clear." The rest seemed to me to be trumped-up nonsense. "Call bets" are common practice and certainly not illegal if properly supervised. Offering membership to hotel porters seemed a questionable practice if abused, and I had stopped it years before.

My experience of Abdul was that he was no worse than any boisterous player, and a suggestion that he had "procured" bunny girls for other members was totally absurd. If proof existed that he had ever done such a thing, he would most certainly have been banned. I knew the rules and so did he.

Finally, as to my friend and fellow director, Clement Freud, I had his personal assurance that he had not taken part in any gambling at our Clubs himself. I saw that the police had mistakenly named him as an "executive" director, whereas in fact Freud was non-executive and—apart from our house rules—legally allowed to gamble.

In my estimation, only Clement Freud was out of line. Because if he had been placing a few bets at the Clermont through a relative or a friend, I had to take the view that he would have been disobeying company wishes. Frank DiPrima asked him to resign. I told him on the phone: "Clement, I have no doubt this will all be cleared up in a few months and you can be reinstated." He accepted the situation and we parted quite amicably.

When I left the office that night I didn't even bother to take the objections with me for the weekend. I had other and far more pleasant things on my mind including a birthday party for a neighbor's daughter, Lucy Black. It was her 21st birthday. Debbie and I spent a totally unconcerned weekend among our guests without the slightest hint of what was going on in London, Los Angeles and, almost without interruption, across the transatlantic cables.

Of course I knew that Frank DiPrima, whom I'd been with in Nassau the week before, was in London. I'd offered to join him for weekend talks. He refused, saying he didn't think it was necessary. I figured that they'd want a more urgent updating.

I hadn't invited any of my Chicago associates to Stocks, and they were staying at the Hilton. It must have been a busy weekend.

Frank DiPrima is a clever lawyer. He is a short, balding man with Coke-bottle glasses. I'd always gotten along well with him until the Nassau meeting when we'd had a squabble over the announcement of my stepping-out from equity participation. It was a small point—I advised delay, to prevent the authorities resisting my arguments while they still felt sorry for me—but we both got a bit heated. Anyway, for reasons already stated, DiPrima was not on my personal guest list.

That weekend, DiPrima met with David Swede, our solicitor. The line between Hefner's Los Angeles mansion and Swede's house was buzzing. The man on the Los Angeles end of the line was Derick Daniels. Had I recognized that this relative newcomer was weighing my situation, I might not have slept so soundly. And I might have started wheels in motion which would at least have got discussions going about the company's future.

I had never considered Derick Daniels a suitable president. He spoke with a Southern drawl, delicate and affected. A slender guy with a mass of curly blond hair, he also has one eye blue and one green. I found him a shade bizarre.

The way he dressed didn't help. He used to appear in silver lamé boiler suits. On more conservative days, he'd wear trousers tucked into cowboy boots with a little scarf tied round his neck. He and his wife were known to some of the Playboy organization as "The Bizarros."

Swede couldn't call on our experienced solicitor and company trustee, Arnold Finer, because Arnold was out of town for a few days. Without my being consulted, inquiries were being put to Gavin Lightman, the barrister who had won our appeal case over the Victoria Sporting Club licence.

But such plots as my colleagues and legal advisers were hatching take time. On Monday when I got to my office I had a call asking me to meet them all on Wednesday afternoon at four "to discuss strategy." Derick Daniels was coming over, I was told.

And still I thought of it only as a routine gathering. Nobody had mentioned Gavin Lightman. I knew nothing of Hefner's personal interest in what was happening. Nor did I know that, on Lightman's advice, Hefner had been informed that the only way Playboy's interests in gaming could be protected—including the casino in Atlantic City—would be to change the London management.

The Wednesday morning meeting was at the offices of the firm of Clifford Turner, Solicitors. They were being eased in as the Playboy solicitors in England since Arnold Finer was approaching retirement age. The elevator took us up to the fifth floor where we were shown into a large conference room. A polished table, large enough to seat thirty people, stretched down the length of the room. The first thing I noticed was that the curtains over the windows were drawn and a very complex telephone with a dial and speaker system stood on a sideboard.

Derick Daniels was wearing a white suit. Even before I came through the door I'd seen another odd thing. His secretary, a plump woman I knew in Chicago, was strolling down the hall outside. That's funny, I thought. None of us takes his secretary with him overseas, on anything but the most crucial trips.

He and Frank DiPrima were sitting down one minute and standing up and moving around the next. Everybody seemed to be nervous. I was surprised to see Gavin Lightman, but greeted him cheerfully. He knew I held him in high regard.

Then I spotted Marv Huston. For some reason I hadn't expected to see him there. I said, "Gee Marv, you turn up on all the fun occasions. Like Nassau."

He looked embarrassed but I had no idea why. In fact, unknown to me, he was the new chairman of Playboy-London. That hadn't been left for a decision at this meeting; it was already decided.

There was a good deal of fidgeting around while Daniels and Lightman held muttered conversations at the far end of the table. I wondered when the meeting was going to start. Then Daniels said to me. "We appreciate your having stepped aside from the Atlantic City deal, Victor, but there is something else Hefner feels you should do, or rather not do. We don't want you to show up for the opening."

Well, I thought, whyever not? Once they got the license to operate gaming there, the best interests of the company would surely be served by having me on the bridge when we launched the ship. I said as much.

"I think you're handling this all very badly," I said. "For me not to show up at the opening of a thing I created—and this was my baby, my brainchild—might look to some people like an admission of guilt. Or as if the corporation was ashamed of its Club president."

I'm not altogether sure how they circled that one. I think Daniels said something about how the press would be "all over you, Victor," and that this would annoy Hef.

None of it sounded very convincing to me. And people were still moving around, coming and going from the room. Also, John Wintle had been headed off and taken somewhere else. I was alone.

There didn't seem to be any real meeting going on. It was more a free-ranging peripatetic discussion. Over the weekend there had been a fair amount of publicity about Clement Freud. They wanted to know about that and I told them.

Freud had resigned. But I said we would reinstate him when we get his matter clarified and the licenses renewed. There were a few shifty looks.

The next thing I clearly remember is that Daniels seemed to lose patience. He got up, sat down, and then said in his slow, Southern voice: "As a matter of fact, Victor, the feeling is that these objections the police have put in against your Clubs are going to cause us a lot of unwanted trouble. We know Bill Gerhauser has been handling all that side for you, and we think he should resign."

I said, "But that's ridiculous. Bill had nothing to do with the objections. He's been in Florida since he was in the Bahamas with me. I have absolute confidence in him. Why should he resign?"

There was some nervous laughter and a few comments. I thought they meant that Bill's resignation would be a temporary thing, although even that was idiotic.

"You know, Victor, it was the Atlantic City authorities who insisted we ask you both to step aside temporarily. That's very significant," Daniels told me.

"That's not very significant," I said. "It was merely pending the outcome of the London problems."

Nobody seemed to want to say much more for the moment and I

started taking them to task. "I haven't done anything wrong," I said. "You're treating me as if I was some sort of threat to the organization."

Daniels interposed brusquely. "As a matter of fact, Victor, the feeling is that you should step out."

Nobody was laughing now, and I could hardly believe the words he said. "You've got to be joking! You really want me and Bill to step out? Who's going to run the gaming—you?"

There was a moment of silence.

"Does Hefner know about this?" I asked.

Daniels nodded. Then he pointed to the telephone on the sideboard. "Call him," he said.

There was no need. I knew Daniels well enough to know that he wasn't bluffing. The thing was too important. Somewhere in his mansion, shielded from confrontation and well away from the sight of blood, my old friend Hugh Hefner had called for my execution.

A picture of the last time I had seen Hef flashed into my mind. He was standing at the pinball machine in California smoking his pipe. I turned to Daniels and said: "I'm not going to call that pinball wizard. You obviously brainwashed him before you came out here."

He didn't respond but shoved a piece of paper in front of me. "You have half an hour to sign this," he said. "It allows you to resign."

"You've got to be kidding," I told him. "Why would I resign? You're firing me. And I want the public to know you're firing me."

I felt a blaze of anger. "Take your paper away," I shouted at him. "And don't get your nose so close to my left fist—I'm lefthanded!"

He didn't react at all. He got up, an over-dressed little whacko in his white Palm Beach suit, and sauntered out of the room without another word.

The rest is a blur. I do know they asked me to attend a directors' meeting to "put all the stuff in place." I was still furious. I said: "Absolutely not! You fired me. I only work for pay, and I'm no longer on your payroll."

Incredibly, the yoyos wanted me to take part in voting for my own dismissal.

Some time later I spoke to Bill on the telephone. "Bill, we've been fired," I told him. He sounded almost relieved. "I'm not a bit surprised," he told me. "In my opinion they've been out to get us for a long time."

And Gavin Lightman? Daniels had told me they'd used him to justify firing me. Was it true? I asked Lightman.

He nodded assent. "I recommended they change the management team."

I said: "*You* recommended it? You surely mean you echoed their desire to change it?"

"No, no, I'd never do that," he said. "Don't accuse me of that. I never give anyone else's opinion when it's my opinion. And it is my opinion."

I said: "Wow! Gavin, you have so little experience in real life. I've been a loyal employee of the company for twenty-six years and you suggested they fire me without even a discussion or investigation?"

I left the meeting. It was about 5:30 p.m.

There was quite a stir in the corridors. Daniels had apparently arrived in London with a press release already written and it had been distributed to the press while this meeting was going on.

My chauffeur was waiting outside. "You're not going to believe this," I told him. "I've just been fired."

I was in a state of shock. I still couldn't accept that it had happened. I was numb. When he drove to the familiar doorway of the Playboy Club the press was there waiting to photograph me with my tie pulled loose, my shirtcollar unbuttoned.

They wanted to know what I thought. And I told them: "In my opinion, they're really dumb. They're acting like idiots."

Inside I told everyone the same thing, even the switchboard girls. Debbie was waiting for me upstairs, and the news shocked her almost as much as it had me; but she tried to calm me.

I put a call through to Hef. He wouldn't take it. I was told: "Mr. Hefner is off the property."

If he had taken my call I don't know what I would have said to him, but it wouldn't have been very nice.

I hardly remember the rest of the evening. I think I had some food sent up for us to eat in the flat. I kept taking calls from newsmen who wanted to know my reaction. They were calling from everywhere, America included.

Sometime that evening I took Debbie over to the Clermont, because I knew they were all there, Huston and the others. And I still felt as though I were some part of Playboy.

Also, I wanted to talk about my agreement with Playboy. On leaving the company, it barred me from going into the gaming business in Great Britain for a further three years. Would I be relieved of that restriction? It suddenly became very important to find out.

They were all there—DiPrima and Huston, with some of the managers from the Clubs. I tried to be as natural as possible and sat down with them. What were the chances, I asked, of my being released from that clause in my contract? They would think about it, Huston said. With a sinking feeling, I knew what that meant.

Angrily, I got to my feet. "You're a collection of assholes," I told them. Then I turned on my heel and walked out. Today I realize that I was being too emotional. But who could blame me at the time? That morning, I was the Bunny King of Britain, the highest-paid executive in England. I had a fleet of Rolls-Royces to take me wherever I wanted to go. I had the use of a penthouse on Park Lane and more than half a million dollars a year in salary and bonus.

That night, when I took a sleeping pill and went to bed, I was just another one of Britain's growing army of unemployed.

Chapter Eleven
PARADISE LOST

I had learned a little about dogs. I know a bit about horses and something about bunnies. A scapegoat was a new sort of animal to me and I was about to learn about scapegoats first hand and in depth.

Bill Gerhauser and I felt sure we could have handled the objections to the renewal of our licences. It all seemed so much simpler than the Victoria case we'd won on appeal the previous October. We believed that the allegations against us were either idle, false rumors put about by adversaries, or technical violations that could be legally justified. We suspected the police and the Gaming Board had wanted all this publicly aired so that no one would feel that Playboy got special treatment.

So why do you suppose Playboy's Chicago administrative executives picked this time to move in on us and end our careers with Playboy?

The answer seemed to lie in their own declining profits. Stepping into our shoes would give them a reason for existing. In my address to the Playboy staff in London after we'd won the Victoria case appeal, my words sounded remarkably hollow. As reported in the *Financial Times:* I said, "Not only has the court underscored Playboy's reputation for the highest standard of integrity. More important, everyone who works in casinos has been assured that

171

their livelihoods need not be put at risk by the greed and dishonesty of a few men at the top."

Everyone, that is, except me. I never thought I'd have to be concerned about company politics. Well, now I knew that my belief in candor, truth and honesty made me seem like a lollipop to some of the people in Chicago.

We had done nothing wrong. And by "we," I mean Playboy. For Derick Daniels and the others to take the public action they did was to suggest that we were in separate camps. They were the good guys and we were the bad. Yet Playboy was the company which employed us all.

Even now, it seems crazy. Playboy was committing suicide on stage for the world to see.

In London we had stood up against Ladbroke. We had opened our files and our casinos to every police and Gaming Board inspection whenever required. Ladbroke shredded its records. We did not. When Ladbroke's marketing director, Andreas Christensen, was arrested in Denmark for three murders and two bank robberies early in 1982, I wondered if Hefner reflected on what he did.

Instead of proudly supporting us as heroes, they treated us as scapegoats. They virtually said: "We're throwing these people out because you say they have broken the law." Maybe it made them feel that by our sacrifice they would appear in some sort of better light at the vital New Jersey hearings. Some hope!

Throughout the long and involved hearings of Playboy-Elsinore Associates' application for the Atlantic City casino license, the British Gaming Board's refusal to renew the London gaming licences was a matter of prime concern. By throwing away the excellent chance of my reversing those licence refusals on appeal (as I had done with the Victoria Sporting Club), Playboy, in effect, pleaded guilty.

Sour grapes? Not at all. On January 3, 1982, I voluntarily gave a sworn deposition to officials of the State of New Jersey Division of Gaming Enforcement. I met the Deputy Attorney for New Jersey in Chicago and answered his questions as fully and truthfully as I knew how. I told him: "I was watching something that had taken me eighteen years to build up. First it was destroyed and then its remnants were sold for a pittance. It was very sad and I was very sad."

At times my lawyer tried to stop me saying so much, but I wanted to clarify my position. About some of the technical objections to cashing checks in our casinos raised by the police in London, I explained: "We had gotten counsel's opinion as to whether this was legal. [In] counsel's opinion it was."

I told the officials, "I don't want you to get the impression that Playboy never did anything wrong. We made mistakes. It was wrong when we allowed hotel porters to be honorary members and bring in customers. We did something wrong when we allowed people to come in the following morning to make good on checks drawn against non-existent bank accounts.

"[But] as soon as these things were discovered they were stopped immediately.

"Not when we got letters from the Gaming Board. Not when *Private Eye* reported we were doing things wrong. Not when a policeman had his foot in the door. We were correcting things as we found them, and I think that is the way the company is and does operate."

They asked me: "In your relations with him over twenty-six years, was Mr. Hefner the type that would panic?"

I said: "Well, I think that if he—yes, I think in the sense that if he thought that maybe somebody was accused of doing something wrong, he would be quick to assume that that must be the case."

Finally I talked about what Playboy may have lost. "I want to make this clearly a part of the record," I said. "I think that Playboy made a great mistake in not going on with the appeal. I think they also made a great mistake not calling [to the Caxton Hall hearing in September last when they lost the licences] myself, Bill Gerhauser and . . . a number of people who had been fired or had resigned over this . . . I could have won the thing."

Hef, if you're reading this, let me repeat that sentence: I could have won the thing.

"So you think Playboy would have won the case?"

I said: "Yes. The thing that frightened Playboy . . . as Hefner said at the annual board meeting—'We're in a Catch 22 situation.' They had done the one thing that they had assured the Gaming Board that they would never do, which is try to control the gaming from abroad. And they had broken the Trust agreement with the Gaming Board. I think that's very tragic."

I still think so. But on the morning of Thursday, April 16, 1981, when I had shaken off the muzzy effects of the sleeping pill I had taken on the night of my firing, my feelings were a lot stronger. I reached my old office alternating between anger and doubt. By now the entire staff knew what had happened. People I'd worked with for years came to me trying to be supportive.

My loyal associates at Playboy were offering to fling themselves in the path of an oncoming train while I stood on the platform with four to five million dollars in my pocket. They had mortgages to meet, while I had a fine house in the country, a $280,000 apartment in Colorado and the house my mother lived in in Spain. I also had the use of the Playboy penthouse, but that—as I was rudely told— would end in a few hours.

"Difficult," I said. I had several of my own pieces of furniture in the place; and the pictures on the walls, some of them quite valuable, all belonged to me. As an act of great clemency, DiPrima finally agreed to let me stay overnight, and even arranged for a truck to take my things to Stocks on Friday morning.

As I left, the switchboard girls gave me a tearful send-off. One bunny, whom I'd dated quite often, was in floods of tears. There were quite a few emotional scenes, though personally I was too numb inside to feel much. Only one thing moved me. As I walked out of the office for the last time, Frank DiPrima had the gall to say: "Have a nice weekend." I felt the urge to punch him on the jaw. I controlled myself.

It was an odd coincidence that my birthday and Good Friday fell on that Friday, April 17. As far as my birthday was concerned, it provided a release. I involved myself in arrangements for a party which had been planned weeks before. Some instinct—perhaps a trace of playboy *sang-froid*—made me join in the revels until exhaustion overtook me. I lasted through half the party, then went upstairs and fell asleep.

Quite a big crowd was staying the weekend at Stocks. When I woke up, I had to consider that from now on their entertainment, for which I had previously paid only one-tenth and the company the rest, was my expense. The running cost of Stocks was at least $600,000 a year.

Playboy owned 36 per cent of the house, and one of the things I had to reckon with was that on leaving the company I would have to buy them out, or let them force me to sell out.

Basically, I saw that I would have to get along on something like a half a million dollars a year. Once my six per cent of the Atlantic City scheme was repaid and re-invested, and including the three years on half pay, which my contract guaranteed, that would be my income. I'd have coffee and doughnut money.

What really mattered was that my whole identity was being taken from me. I was as widely known in England as Hefner was in the United States. Only in one sense were we still connected. I was a trustee of the English Trust we had set up to overcome the Gaming Board's dislike of foreign ownership. Clement Freud and I were both trustees, with Lord Hirschfield and Arnold Finer. By totally ignoring the Trust in firing me, Playboy had shown how brazenly they were prepared to ignore this arrangement.

But Hefner, in his California mansion, was protected from such considerations. Amost hysterical over the threat to the London licences, he had put in a telephone call to Morgan Mason, son of the British film star James Mason, in the White House Press Office. Did Mason know anyone he could suggest to take our places as trustees of the London gaming operation?

I never heard what came of that. But some weeks later, Frank DiPrima declared to the magistrates at Caxton Hall, during the Playboy licence hearings, that "we do not consider we breached the Trust." He also announced that the Trust would continue with Michael Luke as the new chairman and John Venney, Edward

Barnes, and Lord Hirschfield. Clement Freud and I had been replaced—but not until a month after I was fired.

These actions lay ahead. For the time being I wanted only to get away as far as possible from the agony of it all. My house in Spain was empty. It seemed a good place to go for a little sunshine in what had suddenly become a dark and unhappy existence. Debbie and some other friends joined me.

Not long afterwards I was in the Playboy building in Chicago clearing up some loose ends. As the lift doors opened on the seventh floor, where I was waiting to descend, I came face-to-face with Derick Daniels on his way up. Let me repeat, I was going down and he was going up. But as things have been since I left the company, with V.P. Don Parker leaving in March 1982 and other moves forecast, I wondered how long, and how fast, his ascendancy would continue.

I soon found out. Derick Daniels announced his "resignation" at the end of April 1982, and Christie Hefner, Hef's 29-year-old daughter, became president of Playboy Enterprises Inc.

I don't wish my old colleagues ill. While we were working together I had a trust fund set up for my children in America. It legally required eight trustees, and I invited both DiPrima and Marv Huston to take on these roles for me. Though I have since asked them to step down, to avoid embarrassment or confusion, I still value them as people I enjoyed being associated with.

But, having said all that, neither of them has the most elementary knowledge of gaming. If I hadn't been so groggy I would probably have burst out laughing when I saw that one of them became managing director of the entire Playboy gaming operation after I left. That was before the new Trust and Playboy changed their attitude from proud independence to abject respect for the British Gaming Board and their rules in Britain.

On September 14, 1981, the last scene of this Greek drama was played out. Five magistrates—in my experience, usually nice elderly ladies with comparatively little legal training who have somehow earned the title "Justice of the Peace"—gave weighty attention to Playboy's expensive battery of legal talent.

Playboy's handling of this situation was as inept as their previous frantic actions. By now they were giving a passable imitation of a Gilbert and Sullivan farce. An "Admiral of the Queen's Nav-ee" was walking the Playboy quarter-deck, as the new managing director and chief executive of Playboy-Britain. Admiral Sir John Treacher was a fine, distinguished sailor but what he was doing in a gaming casino remained a mystery. Certainly readers of English newspapers found his appointment a stimulating and amusing continuation of Playboy's convulsions.

Sir John signed a three-year employment contract, for exactly half what my overall salary had been—$250,000 a year.

Eight weeks later Sir John was paraded before the magistrates in Caxton Hall as the new face of Playboy in Britain. The press had a field day. The idea that a top-ranking sailor with no gaming experience could steer Playboy's scuttled ship through the legal straits was laughable. But Admiral Treacher made no secret of his belief that gaming experience is not vital in running a casino.

The verdict was delivered: renewal of Playboy Club and Clermont Club licenses was refused. Playboy was assessed the joint costs of the police and Gaming Board amounting to nearly $200,000. Perhaps Sir John realized that the authorities were not impressed enough with his credentials.

When Sir John's new associates reacted to this with a frantic search for someone—anyone—who would buy out Playboy's British interests, he may have wondered what he had gotten into. In the month following the Caxton Hall verdict, on October 5, 1981, Trident Television agreed "in principle" to buy Playboy-Britain for 34 million dollars.

The rest of the tragic story goes from bad to worse. The hearing of the appeal against the magistrates' refusal to renew the casino licenses was set for January 25, 1982. In the same month after Playboy withdrew six million dollars, Trident TV reduced its offer by six million. Sir James Hanson and his Hanson Trust colleagues, Sir Gordon White and millionaire Charles Sweeney paid about $28,000,000 for the entire package. And Playboy settled, like lambs or—should I say—cuddly bunnies.

Shares in Playboy Enterprises, Inc., which had fallen in value by nearly a third on the day after my dismissal, were depressed still further by this sacrifice sale. With the profits I had achieved from the gaming, Playboy's British holdings had been valued at around one hundred million dollars.

When the Chicago yoyos expressed their panic, the stockholders took a beating. And Admiral Sir John Treacher was forced to abandon ship after—again at the stockholders' cost—a very expensive ride. In the six months of his command, his take-home pay, including his redundancy money, worked out at approximately $7,500 a day.

Trident TV, of course, did everything possible to free themselves from Playboy's mismanagement image. The famed London landmark of Playboy's illuminated bunny sign over Park Lane would vanish. No longer would bunny girls conduct members to the gaming tables, or the restaurant. Under Trident TV, "ladylike girls in evening dress" would take their place. And an ex-Scotland Yard chief, Peter Nievens, would direct security within the clubs.

So what was left for Playboy? The company executives still had an urgent need to convince the State of New Jersey authorities that they were fit people to run a multi-million-dollar casino operation in Atlantic City. Like balloonists losing height, Daniels, DiPrima, Huston and Co. had thrown out everything possible—including their most profitable sphere of operation.

Shortly before the hearing of the appeal by Playboy in London in early 1982, I was asked if I bore Hefner any grudge for his treatment of me. Did I think Playboy would win its appeal? I said: "Yes. The issues are all technical. I believe the case has to be argued more vigorously than it was in the first instance."

Speaking of Hefner, I added: "I feel I've been badly wronged by the company. And I feel that the company has done itself a major wrong at the same time. But I'm not a vindictive person and if there is anything I can do to help them in this situation, I am willing to help."

In February 1982, the reality was that Playboy in London was indeed breathing its last, and Atlantic City looked less than promising. A club owner who had been a regular visitor and friend of ours in London, Peter Stringfellow, threw a farewell disco party for the bunnies and me. Marilyn Cole, who had shared so much of the stress of the last few months, was my partner for the evening and, sad as the occasion was, we toasted the future.

Let no one doubt that I walked away from the Playboy empire with a clean sheet. If they don't, I think they should consider both what I have set down in this book and the fact that, unlike some other casino operators in Britain, my integrity has never been and never will be brought into question in court. In Playboy's case no actions were ever taken against me or *anyone* in the company.

Confirmation of the significance of this point recently came from an unexpected source when I happened to run into one of the Playboy lawyers on a flight from London to Chicago. I think he summed it up rather neatly. "You're in fine shape, Victor. Nobody believes you did anything wrong. It's Playboy who will have to learn how much of a paradise they have lost."

If they want to start, they might try looking at the Gaming Board's Annual Report for 1981 which underlines, in rather subtle fashion, the difference between the problems which faced Playboy and those confronting the other casinos which received challenges to their licenses. The paragraphs in the Gaming Board's Report are numbered:

136. Raided . . . Knightsbridge Sporting Club . . . Six principals were subsequently charged...
137. Olympic Casino . . . Raid . . . charges were laid against two directors and three other persons...
138. Certain charges arising from the police raid on casinos of the Coral Group still remain to be heard. [There were subsequently three convictions.]

But paragraph 135 clearly states: "Police and the Board's inspectors executed warrants at the Playboy Club and the Clermont Club. *There were no criminal charges arising...*" (my italics). It should be remembered, too, that in the previous year there had been charges against some of Ladbroke's key personnel and against Victoria Sporting Club principals (before Playboy's takeover).

No charges were made against Playboy directors or staff. Why? As Group Captain Steve Stephens of the British Casino Association noted when I mentioned this subtle commendatory distinction to him, "Victor, there were no charges against Playboy because there were no charges." Of course, I know that, but I liked the way he put it!

I think it's a tragedy that the "game" of casino enforcement can, even at magistrates' level, bring about the cancellation of a licence for offences or technical violations that don't merit the filing of charges against anybody. Something's wrong. It's like a situation where all crimes, from murder to parking violations, are subject to the death penalty—even parking violations where the "no parking area" isn't clearly delineated and posted.

Chapter Twelve

TAKING STOCK: AN EPILOGUE

Two years have passed since that rainy day in April 1981 when Hugh Hefner, my good friend for more than twenty-seven years, supported the decision of his top executives from Chicago, to "change management" of the London operations.

"Change management" was the euphemism for firing the fellow who, time after time, had been instrumental in pulling the company out of its most difficult jams.

In April 1982, Playboy was refused a permanent license for its Atlantic City casino unless Hefner resigned and disposed of his interest in Playboy Enterprises. It was quite a slap in the face.

There was a clear parallel between what happened in London and what happened in New Jersey. Hefner was being disqualified, because of something which should have been perceived as a credit to him and to the Playboy organization.

Just as Playboy had gotten into trouble in England because it stood up to Ladbroke's threats, so Playboy in New Jersey was being punished for an incident that had occurred twenty-one years earlier when Hefner had played a hero's role in exposing the extortion practiced by New York State's Liquor Authority chairman.

On the day Hefner was refused a license for Atlantic City I wired him from my apartment in Aspen, Colorado, where I was writing this book and enjoying some spring skiing.

I said, "Hef, I think it is horrible that you have been falsely damned over the New York extortion case. I know how disheartening such a situation can be. I will do whatever I can to help you set the record straight."

Indeed, I knew well how disheartening it could be to have one's integrity impugned.

On May 10, 1982, Trident itself, using much the same legal team that had presided over the Playboy debacle, was not only denied a new license to the London Playboy Club but the judges explained their refusal with the assertion that Trident had not shown that it was "fit and proper" to run the casino.

Three days later, demonstrating the whimsicality of the South Westminster licensing system, different justices from the same bench granted Trident a license to run the Clermont.

Trident, which wasn't "fit and proper" on Monday had become fit and proper on Thursday!

To those of us like Bill Gerhauser and myself who built Playboy in England, it's all very sad. We had become scapegoats where no scapegoats were needed.

Even good friends misunderstood the nature of the objections to Playboy's licenses. When the magistrates refused to renew they told each other, "Victor must have done something wrong or encouraged others to do something wrong."

Not true. I never did. I never could.

As Playboy's Andy Wheeler, for many years our casino controller, said to me just recently: "Victor, we would have won that license case in a walk. Why didn't they let us?"

You've got to explain it to me sometime, Hef. Why didn't you let us?

Hefner's California mansion was bought for one million. Playboy poured another nine million into it—much of the money from the British casino operation. It paid for the more than $2,000,000 "to bring Mr. Hefner's offices and personal quarters up to standards." It paid for the hot tubs and the two movie screens and the $60,000 worth of monkeys, rabbits and birds.

Max Kingsley, Managing Director of Sportsman Limited, the only other major British casino company, is considered one of the shrewdest men in the gaming industry. When I was fired he wrote to me saying, "Quite apart from showing an incredible lack of appreciation for your efforts over so many years, it seems to me that Playboy's decision can do nothing but harm in their efforts to retain the licenses. I find it difficult to believe that such a decision could have been arrived at by anyone with any real depth of understanding of the British gaming scene."

Difficult, indeed!

The eight-story building on Park Lane, between the Dorchester and the Hilton Hotels, once housed the most profitable casino in the world. London's Playboy produced a larger profit than Las Vegas's Caesars Palace.

The building that once proudly flew two Union Jacks, the Stars and Stripes, and Playboy's distinctive orange and black bunny insignia from flagpoles on the roof is now flagless and dark.

The eighty-one betting shops around London that were handsomely decked out in Playboy's orange and black colors under their storefront sign, "Playboy Bookmakers," now await redecoration with a "now under the management of William Hill" poster in their windows.

The bunny is gone from London.

When Derick J. Daniels, the Playboy president, jetted to London to hand me my walking papers, he underlined the finality of my firing by announcing to the press, "He ain't coming back ... no way!"

I suspect, however, that in a way I did come back to haunt him. For when he removed me, he killed the casinos. Their loss devastated Playboy.

Thus, inevitably, his action cost him his own job.

On April 28, 1981, Hefner announced Daniels' "resignation."

Poor Derick. The undertaker had dug his own grave. And seems to be so deeply buried in it that recently he sent out cards to his friends which said, "Derick Daniels is alive and well and living in Chicago."

Lots of luck.

How has Playboy fared?

Playboy, which made $30 million in the year ending June 30, 1981, lost more than $51 million in the year ending June 30, 1982. This was a swing of more than $80 million dollars.

Eighty million dollars!

I wonder if Hefner ever asks himself, as he surveys the wreckage, "Why didn't I trust Victor to solve the problems in Britain?"

On occasion I have asked myself why I didn't get on a plane and fly to Los Angeles for a face-to-face with Hef. I would have explained clearly what a mistake he was making both for me and, perhaps more important, for the future of Playboy.

I didn't, and that was that. I must content myself with the reminder that I wasn't myself. I hadn't fully recovered from the fractured skull from the horseback riding accident. My energy level was low. And my execution came with such swiftness and as such a surprise that I was in a state of shock.

Had I taken that plane, I have no doubt that things would be different today.

But life is full of "it might have beens," so there is little point in dwelling on that one.

Derick Daniels received termination pay totaling $476,000. Admiral Sir John Treacher, no relation to the actor, received $740,000 in termination money—or enough for quite a supply of fish and chips. W. Russell Barry joined Playboy as a vice president in August 1980. He worked two years of a three-year contract and received $400,000 in termination pay.

And poor Hef didn't have a dime for a phone call to me.

Playboy's 1,700 employees and 27,000 stockholders got one good break. Christie Hefner, Hef's bright, charming and extremely pretty daughter is now president of the company. Had she replaced Derick Daniels a year earlier, things might have developed into a different scenario. I have the feeling that she would have given me the courtesy of a face-to-face discussion. Perhaps Christie can rejuvenate the bunny after all.

I hope so.

Playboy now has big hopes for its pay TV cable service. The magazine certainly needs help: it's losing circulation and advertising. But Playboy has had a couple of breaks. For example, the building that houses the New York Playboy Club, which I bought for $650,000, was recently sold for more than $10,000,000.

Others are not so optimistic. Value Lines, the stock advisory service, tells its readers to "avoid these shares..."

The carrot sticks aren't coming from London and the magazine is getting slimmer and slimmer. Is Playboy coming to life again or is this the last bunny hop?

How has Victor Lownes fared?

Not badly, thank you. I don't have to send out postcards saying that I'm alive and well. From my years at Playboy, I had saved and invested more than four million dollars. Add to this my severance pay from Playboy, of some $250,000 a year for three years.

I have the apartment in Aspen, a house in Marbella, and I've bought a nice house in London, in Chelsea. And, of course, I have my beautiful home, Stocks.

Yes, I still have Stocks. Recently I enjoyed turning it into a successful conference center and party venue. Its indoor and outdoor pools, games rooms, squash and tennis courts, horses, discotheque, and full complement of audio visual and motion picture equipment make it ideal for the purpose.

I enjoyed sharing my forty-two room mansion with Playboy's bunny training school, and I like sharing it with other company groups. Making Stocks self-sufficient was essential if I planned to keep it.

Not long ago one of London's trendiest up-market night clubs, Wedgie's, came up for sale. I grabbed it. Michael Wield is the designer who had enhanced many of the rooms at Stocks and at the Playboy Club. It was he who had sole responsibility over the years for keeping the Clermont Club's ambience accented as the most elegant of all London's gaming clubs. I've worked with him to redo Wedgie's. When we're finished, it will be renamed "Stocks."

It will be "Stocks in Town" and will be coupled with "Stocks in the Country" so that our members will have both a town club and a country club for their entertainment. (Although members have to be both sponsored and seconded by established members of Stocks Club, we'll make a special exception in the case of American readers kind enough to have bought this book! Send your application to Stocks Club, 107 King's Road, London SW3. We're offering a special temporary Stocks membership for American visitors to London.)

This may all be anticlimactic after being listed in the *Guinness Book of Records* as the highest-paid executive in the UK, but I can still afford an afternoon tea for two.

My solid financial position sometimes makes it difficult to explain to people how deeply hurt I've been because of the intangible things I've lost: job satisfaction, pride of accomplishment, genuine day-to-day happiness and, most important of all, an untarnished reputation for honor and integrity.

But they're returning, and by now it's obvious to everyone concerned that it was something of a disaster for Playboy to remove me.

That's for Hefner to dwell upon.

Me? I'm looking at new opportunities, new ideas, new plans ...

Keep an eye on the *Guinness Book of Records* for future developments.

INDEX

187